ACPL ITEM
DISCARDED

ANNEX

ANNEX

S0-BWV-402

Date		
31 Jul '39	APR	3
3 Oct '39	27 Sep '4	
11 Jan '40	27 Oct '4	
11 Mar '40	8 Dec '4	
11 May '40	19 Mar	
8 Aug '40	5 Oct '40	
14 Nov '40	23 Sep '4	
27 Nov '	3 May '4	
	17	
13 Jan '41		
20 Mar '41	29 Ma	
DEC 3 0 1941		
15 Apr '42	25 Fe	
7 May '42	13 Mar	
27 Apr '43	23 Ja	
19 Oct '43	9	

JOHANN SEBASTIAN BACH

A. 7/18

SYMPHONIC MASTERPIECES

BY
OLIN DOWNES

785. 11
D75

1935 · *The Dial Press* · NEW YORK

E. C. SCHIRMER MUSIC CO.,
221 Columbus Ave.,
Boston, Mass.

COPYRIGHT, 1935,
BY
THE DIAL PRESS, INC.

PRINTED IN THE UNITED STATES OF AMERICA
BY THE STRATFORD PRESS, INC., NEW YORK

280902

TO MY MOTHER

Who made possible my experiences of music,
apropos of many concerts we have
enjoyed together

OCT 23 1935

ACKNOWLEDGMENTS

CERTAIN of the introductory paragraphs of the chapter on Wagner appeared originally in the *New York Times* and are here reprinted with the *Times'* permission.

The thematic quotations from César Franck's Symphony in D minor are taken from Daniel Gregory Mason's arrangement and editing of the work for piano solo (Music Lovers' Symphony Series, No. 6), published by G. Schirmer, Inc., and are used in this book by permission of the publishers, owners of the copyright.

The thematic quotations from the C. F. Peters Edition of the arrangement for piano solo of Richard Strauss's "Till Eulenspiegel" are used by permission of the copyright owner, C. F. Peters. From the same publishers' edition come the quotations from Beethoven's Fifth Symphony.

The quotations from Mozart's G minor symphony are from the arrangement edited by John Marshall, in the Boston University Edition, published by Charles W. Homeyer & Company.

CONTENTS

CONTENTS

CONTENTS

[xi]

CONTENTS

QUOTATIONS

ILLUSTRATIONS

INTRODUCTION

I LIKE to remember the first time I heard an orchestra.

How could I forget? This took place on a winter
afternoon in New York City, when I, fifteen years of
age, had trudged shivering through the snow to take
a lesson at Mrs. Jeannette M. Thurber's National
Conservatory of Music. The Conservatory was an old
building downtown, one which impressed me as having been converted from a private house to educa-
tional uses. It had in my eyes, at any rate, a fine gloom
and a warm hospitality. I can never forget what happened when I reached this haven. The door, closing
behind me, shut out the whine of the wind and in-
stantaneously replaced this sound with another which
fell on my ears as wondrous transmutation of the
music of the elements. It was the sound of an orchestra. I know now what was being played. It was the
beautiful second theme of Beethoven's early and Mo-
zartian piano concerto in C major. But the effect of
violins singing that theme over the stormy splendor

of the ensemble was to me like a god's instrumentation of the tempest.)

Then, with some soloist or other, they played the finale of the Bruch G minor violin concerto. So far as I was concerned, the finale of "Götterdämmerung" could have been no more overwhelming. And then I learned, to my considerable astonishment, that it was the Conservatory orchestra rehearsing, and that if I wanted more of that wonder I had only to open a door and enter. Great fortune was with me, for I opened the wrong door and I emerged, not in front but inside of the orchestra. I was just in back of two immense double-basses, those deep-breathing lungs of the ensemble, and I remember my surprise, in observing second violinists not far away from me vigorously making tremolos which, near as I was to them, were inaudible in the magnificent commotion. And there, facing me over an array of players and instruments, stood Leo Schultz, whose face seemed very much like Beethoven's, conducting, and "shushing" with two fingers to his lips for a better balance. Then the orchestra swept up to a climax, which, indeed, was marvel past the telling.(It was as if one had dived deep in an ocean of tone, and the swirling clamoring waters had met overhead. Coral caves, gleaming pearls, sporting mermaid and leering monster would not have carried greater enchantment!)

I suppose nothing ever quite equals the effects of such early impressions. And yet—I don't know—to

[xiv]

me the orchestra remains supreme magic, an incomparable triumph of man, a god-like transmutation which merges seen and unseen in terms of a transcendent beauty. For consider—what are the gross materials of which the orchestra is made? They are bits of wood, metal, animal tissue. These substances the magician man endows with a curious power and through them releases the secrets of nature from which they came. They sing with strange and hypnotic voices, sounding dramas of tone beyond mortal experience. They companion the proudest dreams, the uttermost reaches of the spirit. For it is not the sounds alone which move you, said Whitman; it is their exquisite meanings—the things of which you are reminded by the instruments.

But it is not easy to relate these experiences. It is even dangerous to attempt to do so. The principal difficulty arises from the fact that it would take a thousand poets and savants in one to convey by words anything adequate about the most intangible and mysterious of the arts. The danger is great because it is so easy to mislead the reader and misrepresent the composer by discovering in his score meanings he never intended.

Nevertheless, the sum of a work of art is not only its creation; it also lies in its interpretation—the creative response of the individual to whom the work appeals. And that individual is you or I. It is not a question of our significance or omniscience

[xv]

either. It is a question of the response to a master-piece, individually and collectively, by a community. Shakespeare, let us say, is not only Shakespeare. He is the sum of humanity's interpretation of him. Something is given Shakespeare, is added to his stature, by the thoughts that we, in exchange for his great wisdom, have showered upon him. He is himself, multiplied by us. The same principle holds true of any form of art and any individual in whom that art awakens a response. We listen to Beethoven or Debussy. We listen and we have to interpret, articulately or otherwise. It is well that we do so and fruitful that we exchange our ideas. The interpretations of a work of art are as varied as the minds and natures of those to whom it speaks. Each of us sees the work in a different light and each from his own point of view approaches nearer the common truth. Therefore, every man to his interpretation and I to mine. Art is created by humanity and is answerable to it.

Or put it differently. There stands a mountain. It does not move. The shape of the rocks has not changed perceptibly in a century. Yet those who gaze see a different mountain in the evening than they saw in the morning. If you lived north of the mountain you would never recognize it by the descriptions of those who lived south of it. Nor would a whole lifetime of observation and reflection, or the writings of all the geographers and poets completely reveal the mountain's secret. But the total of your observation and such of their writings as interested you would make you the richer and the more appreciative of your mountain.

There are, of course, those who never want to behold the heights from any other place than the one in which they have always lived. Some of these will even deny that other vistas are possible. Personally I cannot understand how any thinking person can restrict himself to the single point of view. Consider the history of music. In the last three centuries music has swung from one extreme to the other of intent and expression. At the beginning of the Seventeenth century the art experienced a prodigious quickening through its new association with drama in the form of opera. In a later period its predominant characteristic was that of design. The Nineteenth century revolted against formalism, and brought music into intimate relations with other arts. Many did and many do think this a mistaken tendency on the part of composers. Yet it is impossible to deny that music's association in that whole period with poetry, drama, even philosophy, resulted in a particular enrichment of its quality and its literature. In spite of this one can read a hundred books in which the authors insist that music has no actual association with the human adventure; that it is a pure or abstract art consisting in the arrangement of tones of given pitch in terms of rhythm and design, and that the attempt to find any other significance in it is ill-judged and futile.

They may be right! Certainly they are right for themselves, which is all anyone can be. For me music is intimately associated with and inseparable from thinking, feeling, being—the sum of life and man, the *whole* man. Sometimes the relation is obvious, sometimes not. Perhaps it is least obvious when it reflects a pure and impersonal beauty. I do not know. I do not profess to know all the faces of my mountain. Its mystery lures and perplexes me because it is never the same, and I seldom think the same things about it. But I believe that we read books, witness dramas, look at painting and sculpture, and contemplate other forms of art, fundamentally for purposes of discovery and self-realization. From this field of experience I cannot exclude music.

Now each art has a language of its own. To those unfamiliar with its idioms that language may not be immediately comprehensible. My experience is that often a word or sentence is sufficient to connect music and imagination in the mind of the reader, and I find that with a very little aid of this sort the musical perception of the individual and the play of his imagination are stimulated. Then he is off on his own voyage of discovery.

This was forcibly impressed upon me in the course of radio talks that I gave for several seasons about orchestral music. Synopses and amplifications of these talks were the origin of this book, first published under the title of "Symphonic Broadcasts." The present version adds much to the original material, which has been altered and extensively revised, while certain subjects which lay outside the scope of the direct symphonic narrative have been eliminated.

Here, in chronological succession, are discussed the greater number of those symphonic works which hold their place in the contemporary American repertory. A chapter has been added upon the orchestra and musical forms of Bach's time and the book brought to the period of the Stravinsky of "Petrouchka" and "Le Sacre du printemps."

Also included are thematic quotations from four representative compositions which, for those readers interested in such matters, illustrate basic principles and evolutions of symphonic structure. It is not essential for an understanding of the matter in the book that these quotations be consulted, but it is probable that a reader who can play a little on the piano, or has a friend who can do so, will find it interesting, by this means, to take a peek over the composer's shoulder and a glance around his workshop.

Symphonic music has only recently become accessible to the great American public, thanks to the ministrations of radio and of phonograph records, as well as the rapid development of orchestral institutions. To the many new listeners, particularly those whom these conditions have developed, it is hoped that the following pages may be suggestive.

OLIN DOWNES

New York
January 1, 1935.

SYMPHONIC
MASTERPIECES

JOHANN SEBASTIAN BACH

1685–1750

BACH'S small orchestra, which would be called today not a "symphony" but a "chamber" orchestra, was not nearly equal in sonority or variety of tone-tint to our modern body of instruments, but it was more than sufficient for his expressive purposes in the concert-room. This orchestra consisted predominantly of "strings"—instruments, large and small, of the violin family; with flutes, oboes and sometimes a bassoon, for the "woodwind" choir; high trumpets and sometimes a horn or two for the "brass" of the fuller scores; sometimes kettledrums, and in most cases harpsichord to fill out the harmony.

In those days the art of the modern conductor was unknown. The leader of the orchestra, who was often the composer himself, sat at the harpsichord (a keyed instrument, and one of the precursors of the piano), or in the seat of the first violinist, established the tempo, and occasionally by a gesture indicated a change of pace of some other salient feature of the interpretation. But the fine shadings, the blazing rhetoric and tremendous climaxes of which the modern orchestra is capable, and which form so much of the stock in trade of the conductor of today, were absent. Nor had the Bach orchestra great flexibility. It afforded planes, rather than shadings of instrumental tone. One passage would be played softly "piano" and the next loudly—"forte"; perhaps only relatively soft or loud, but without modern mezzo-tints. Contrasts rather than gradations of "piano" and "forte" were the style. The beauty and significance of the music lay in its melody, rhythm and structure. It was a less nervous age than ours. The composition, without, as it were, raising its voice to a dramatic pitch, spoke for itself and with no ulterior meaning. Thus Bach's chamber orchestra was not intended for dramatic effect. It was intended to weave wonderful patterns of pure music.

Bach had a strong sense of the fitness of things. Frequently in pages of his Cantatas and Passions he uses his orchestra for purposes of tone-painting, in accordance with situations suggested by the text. But when he sits down to write for a few instruments ordered music in which purely melodic and rhythmical ideas bud and foliate, as a tree grows from the ground and puts out branches and leaves; when the plenteousness of his invention, the exuberance of his workmanship and his own abounding vitality seize you and make your blood dance in your veins as his motives dance in the orchestra —he communicates an incomparable feeling of health, logic and beauty. You listen and are musically complete. In Bach's music is something profoundly nourishing and lifegiving—something which seems to be in league with basically simple rhythms of the universe, and the pulse and growths of nature.

*   *   *

When Bach wrote in the orchestral forms of his time he was content to use accepted forms and fill the old bottles with the new wine of his genius. The forms in which he wrought so masterfully were principally the suite, or overture—the terms being at the time synonymous—and the concerto. The symphony as we know it today had not yet appeared. The suite was a collection of dance forms based on rhythms which had in previous ages accompanied the actual performances of dancers, or other festivities. The elementary dance forms were then taken by composers of learning and genius as a basis for richer and more varied designs, carried far beyond the point of their origin.

The various dances that made the suite came from different parts of the world and different ranks of society. Nationalism was not yet the influence in music that it became in a later century, and the forms of the suite were of international derivation. Thus the Allemande, a flowing movement in a duple rhythm, purported to come from Southern Germany. The lively Courantes were of two sorts, the one of the

[3]

French, the other of the Italian persuasion. The grave Sarabande was an old Spanish dance; the Gigue was supposed to be of British origin.

The suite was often preceded by a free preluding movement, and the composer, if he chose, could write in other dance measures than those already mentioned —the Gavotte, Bourée, Passepied, Menuet, Polacca or Polonaise—this last a Polish title, though the Polonaise of Bach's B minor suite for flute and strings is far from the form as conceived by Chopin. And there were movements of less exact identification, such as the Air (originally a dance movement in spite of its title and melodic character), and fanciful titles such as "Badinerie," or "Rejouissance"—movements in lighter vein, possibly suggested by the grace and playfulness of certain French compositions of the period. There were different variation-forms. Some were called "doubles." A Sarabande or other dance would be played first in simple outline; the "double" which followed would be the same melody elaborately varied. Grander variation-forms were the Chaconne, or its close relative, the Passacaglia. Of these Bach has left the world two incomparable examples: the Chaconne from the D minor suite, or "partita," for violin alone, and the colossal C minor organ Passacaglia, of which more in a later page. It can be seen from the foregoing that if the amazing effects of the modern orchestra were not yet possible; if Bach reserved his greatest instrumental conceptions for the organ, nevertheless a very considerable variety of musical expression was attainable with a few instruments and in the forms of the old suite—particularly as these forms were developed and sublimated at the hands of the master.

Lastly, to conclude this phase of the subject, we come to those forms of larger dimensions and fewer divisions than the suite, which were ancestors of both the concerto and the symphony of the later period: the concerto for a solo instrument or instruments with orchestra, and—the biggest orchestral form of the day—the concerto grosso. A characteristic of this noble form was the division of the orchestra in two principal parts: a small group of solo players called the "concertino," and the larger ensemble group known variously as the "ripieno" or "tutti" (or, in earlier days—the very title later bestowed upon the forms as a whole—the "concerto grosso"). The splendid possibilities of the concerto grosso lay in the opportunities not only for the development of melodic motives, but the play of both solo and ensemble elements, the march and counter-march of division against division, part against part.

*   *   *

Now all this music was written in the contrapuntal or polyphonic manner. These two terms are similar in their meaning. Counterpoint means literally "point against point," or, in the musical application, note

[5]

against note, or melody against melody. Similarly, music that is polyphonic is "many-voiced." It is made from two or more melodic parts, each of individuality and importance. It is a tonal fabric, its strands harmoniously woven together. Such music is made of "melodic lines" rather than single melodies supported by chords or some equivalent musical background.

The kind of music which gives us a principal melody (usually, though not invariably, in the upper part) supported by chords, arpeggios, or other species of harmonic filling-in, is known technically as "homophonic," or "one-voiced." It may be said that the richest style of composition—that practiced, for example, by Wagner and by other great composers of the nineteenth century—is the one which combines virile polyphony, and harmony, and instrumental color. But fashions change. Some composers today are looking back towards the more strict and linear methods of earlier centuries. Homophonic manifestations were already clear in Bach's time; they were even incipient in certain of his compositions, but they had not yet become general tendencies. Bach stands foursquare to eternity, understanding and assimilating all styles of music, but essentially the incomparable master of centuries of polyphonic development. When he died it was as if humanity were instinctively aware that nothing beyond what he had achieved could possibly be accomplished by his methods. There ensued, swift upon his heels, the virtual abandonment of the polyphonic for the homophonic style, with the result of a revolution in music.

Orchestral Works

Bach left four orchestral suites, for different instrumental combinations. The first one, in C major, is for two oboes, a bassoon and strings. The second one is in B minor, for flute and strings. The third is the suite in D major, with the justly famous Air—that noble and tender melody that the violinist Wilhelmj made popular in his arrangement for the G string. The last suite is in the same key, and, like the third, more heavily scored than the earlier ones. It would be superfluous to describe these suites in detail, while it is not exaggeration to say that each one of them is a mine of strong and beautiful music. The two most frequently played are the delicious second suite, for the flute and strings, and the third, with the celebrated Air already referred to, and other pieces also famous.

These suites and the Brandenburg concertos belong to the time when Bach was concertmaster for the Prince of Cöthen. There he had an orchestra to experiment with, and an employer who was an uncommonly intelligent patron of music. Wherever he went in the course of his hard-working life, Bach took what musical means came to his hand, exploiting to the utmost their possibilities. The Brandenburg concertos are his first attempts at instrumental composition on a big scale. They constitute superb examples of his

[7]

power of synthesis and origination. In them Bach exemplifies all the resources and possibilities of the concerto of his day, while his audacious employment of wind instruments was beyond anything previously attempted.

The opening allegro of the first Brandenburg concerto, in F, is a prototype of many of Bach's fast movements in the pulse and vigor of the music, the glints and contrasts of instrumental color, and the almost cellular development of the ideas. The slow movement, as customary in this form, is the melodic one. It consists largely in a duet of the first oboe and the small, high-pitched violin that Bach selects for his string solo, over the quiet accompaniment and the occasional rejoinder of the lower stringed instruments. The finale, again in a fast tempo, dismisses the more poetical mood of the preceding section by passages of the gayest and most rollicking humor. The rhythms and motives are almost those of the folk-dance. This concerto is quite fully scored for horns, oboes, high violin and the customary other strings.

The first and second Brandenburg concertos are closely related as regards form and in key. Very different from the first, however, and highly ingenious is the color scheme in the second, achieved by combinations between the solo trumpet, solo flute, solo oboe and solo violin, set against the "ripieno" of the other strings. This, figuratively speaking, is Bach with his coat off, in the open air, leading the measure. A rapid florid figure is usually set against a stockier and more energetic movement in another part. Flying passages contrast delightfully with the sustained singing tones of other voices. The sonorous "tuttis" crash in after exhilarating solo displays, as if to say "bravo." With four measures of this music, or even two—such is the divinity of its arithmetic—the listener feels instinctively aware of all that is to come, while, on the other hand, there is such constant germination of the motives that it is certain Bach could have continued for many more pages without exhausting his ideas or our interest. For the slow movement, flute, oboe and violin converse together over a steady moving bass. The finale is a lively and audacious combination of rhythmic figures and the strongly contrasted colors of trumpet, flute, oboe and string tone.

The third Brandenburg concerto has quite a different plan. It uses only strings, and divides the orchestra not in solo and ensemble parts, but in three groups, of equal size, each comprising three violins, violas and cellos. Those players, virtually soloists all, must be stout fellows; the sturdy two-fisted opening movement asks not only a substantial tone but the hearts of men. In modern performance the numbers of players in each choir is proportionately multiplied. The first movement is followed by the shortest slow movement in orchestral music—two measures! Measures which are really only sustained chords to separate the two quick-moving divisions of the work from

[9]

each other. In the last section there is more display of individual part-writing than in the first, two themes flying with nimbleness and legerdemain from group to group of instruments.

The fourth Brandenburg concerto has a first movement scored piquantly for a solo violin, two solo flutes and the "ripieno" strings. At first the strings mark by a sharp stroke the beat, while the flutes carry the lilting tune. Later on come some whirling passages of great velocity for the solo violinist—who must have been a good man, possibly Spiess of the Prince's band, or even Bach himself, for he in his youth was no indifferent executant on the violin as on other instruments. The slow movement is an excellent illustration of the contrasts in planes of sonorities which Bach's instrumental music often affords, and to which reference has already been made. It juxtaposes soft and loud passages which answer each other. Stocky counterpoint, at a vigorous pace, and rapid scale passages that relieve it, make the stuff of the finale.

The fifth Brandenburg concerto, in D major, for performance by solo flute, solo violin and solo harpsichord, is the one which gives prominent display to the keyed instrument. The festive figure that opens the movement is carried along vigorously by the harpsichord (or usually, when it is played in these days, by the piano). There follow various combinations of concertante and "ripieno," with special bravura passages for the harpsichord player, and finally a long and unaccompanied cadenza for that executant which is a masterly summing up of what has preceded, extending almost to the end of the movement. The slow movement is for the polyphonic ensemble. In the finale the harpsichord again takes a prominent part.

The sixth Brandenburg concerto, in B flat, is for solo violas and 'cello, with the strings "ripieno." It begins with a swinging "canon in the unison," one part imitating at the distance of a single beat the motive just played by another part, and so continuing throughout the movement, which, following this precise method, provides the most exhilarating music. The slow movement is the one that is deepest in meaning and the most elaborate in the part-writing of any slow movement of the Brandenburg set. There are four separate and eloquent melodic lines. There is a noble severity of design, profound beauty and feeling. And again, in the finale, Bach's laughter echoes through the world.

Such are a few of the surface characteristics of the Brandenburg concertos. Bach wrote other concertos for solo instruments and orchestra—two concertos for solo violin, and the concerto for two violins; concertos for solo harpsichord, two concertos for two harpsichords and two for three harpsichords, and the quadruple concerto, which is a transcription by Bach of the Vivaldi concerto for four violins with orchestra. Most of these concertos, however, are transcriptions by Bach of concertos for solo violin or for other instruments by other composers. He was all the time absorbing music, any and all music that he deemed worthy of study, and transcribing it. He transcribed for different instruments a great many of his own works. When he transcribed he often developed. When the concertos come from an outside source they are more than copies of other men's music, in many cases constituting improvements on the original which have caused otherwise perishable material to survive and come down to us.

Organ Works in Orchestral Transcription

Some say that Bach's real orchestra was the organ, which gave him resources of volume and color unequaled by any other instrument of his time. He composed for this instrument in an extremely individual way, and with an infinite variety of form and expression.

There are many orchestral transcriptions of the organ works of Bach. Respighi and Stokowski, among others, have arranged various of the chorale-preludes and the C minor Passacaglia.

Each one of the chorale-preludes is a tone-poem, inspired by the meaning of the texts to which the chorales (which formed an integral part of the Protestant service) were sung. Thereupon Bach, seated at the organ, would open the gates of his soul and deliver his own sermon. He would take the original chorale melody and develop its musical possibilities in accordance with the spiritual situation. The immediate purpose was inculcation of the religious sentiment and enrichment of the church ceremonial. But Bach's vast spirit ranged farther than that. Ceremonial was forgotten. The world and the congregation too were forgotten. From the musical essence of the chorale flowered the richest, the most touching, the most mystical manifestations of the spirit of the man to whom, in Schumann's memorable words, music owes a debt as great as that of religion to its founder.

Here is Bach's soul. Here he stands revealed as he never can be by history. For Bach as a personality is distant and legendary, and what exists of history and legend is not particularly romantic. We know that Bach was a singularly honest, industrious and responsible citizen; that he labored gigantically as organist, choirmaster and composer in corners of Germany of the aftermath of the Thirty Years' War; that he married twice, paid his bills, begot twenty children, and compelled his wives to copy his music. We know that he loved good company and good cheer when there was time for these things; that he could be irascible and draw his sword on a recalcitrant bassoonist (a privilege for which others have sighed) ; and, to paraphrase a remark of Lawrence Gilman, that Bach was in the habit of turning out masterpieces as automobiles are turned out from a Ford factory. Granting all this, we do not know Bach the man through history. The whereabouts of his very grave was unknown for a hundred and forty-four years after his death. It might be said that posterity had done him the honor of forgetting him as a man, while cherishing, with always more reverence, gratitude and comprehension, his music.

•

Three Chorale-Preludes

(Transcribed for orchestra by Ottorino Respighi)
I.   Nun komm', der Heiden Heiland
II. Meine Seele erhebt den Herren
III. Wachet auf, ruft uns die Stimme

The three chorale-preludes originally written for organ that Ottorino Respighi selected for orchestral treatment were scored by him in October, 1930, and were performed for the first time anywhere in New York at the Philharmonic-Symphony concerts of October 13, 14, 15 and 16 of the same year. When you hear the first one you sense the tragic and mystical side of Bach's nature. You feel how much he comprehended of human life and sorrow, how lonely he was, and how that great soul fled to its solitudes and its communion with the one friend, guide and counselor, the Lord God.

Lawrence Gilman's program notes on the occasion of the New York première contained an admirable exposition of the nature and contents of the chorales,

[14]

which is partially summarized in the following paragraphs. The first line of the chorale text, which is associated with Luther's Christmas hymn, is, in Dr. Terry's translation, "Come, Redeemer of our Race." Bach has turned the chorale theme into a song of mystical pathos and supplication. The second piece is a transcription of Bach's transcription of the fifth movement of his tenth church cantata, "Meine Seele erhebt den Herren," a cantata known as the "German Magnificat." The thought is of "The power of the Almighty, the dispersal of the enemy, the humbling of the great ones of the earth—these are the outstanding features of the picture painted by the composer." The movement that Bach transcribed for organ was originally a duet for tenor and alto, with the theme of the Magnificat set against it. In Respighi's transcription wind instruments sustain the Magnificat theme. This piece is shorter than the one preceding, and more militant in mood—sterner stuff. The third chorale-prelude also comes from a church cantata, "Wachet auf, ruft uns die Stimme" (Sleepers, awake! A voice is calling"). It is the fourth movement from the cantata, in which the chorale melody is sung by the tenors against orchestral counterpoint. Respighi redistributes the parts in very effective orchestration. The conception is of the calls of the watchmen from the walls of Jerusalem to the Wise and Foolish Virgins, to prepare for the coming of the Heavenly Bridegroom, and the emotions occasioned by these summonses. Bach's counterpoint has the character of a joyous dance. There is the thought of the call of the watchmen, and the procession drawing nearer. The movement develops to a magnificent climax. These are three, and only three, examples of Bach's depth and creative power.

•

Passacaglia and Double Fugue in C minor

(Transcribed for orchestra by Ottorino Respighi, Leopold Stokowski, and others)

The grandest architectonics and fantasy of a staggering sublimity characterize the great Preludes and Fugues and the C minor Passacaglia. This astonishing Passacaglia is in fact one of the mightiest of all Bach's creations, and a wonderful example of a favorite method of musical variation and development in the period before the establishment of the classic symphony. (The Passacaglia has on occasion been incorporated in the symphony.) It is built upon a short, bare theme, eight measures long, fit for the Rock of Ages. It is a theme, incidentally, particularly practical for the foot-work of the organist. On it the composer builds twenty variations and a final fugue. The theme strides through the orchestra, while about it luxuriates Bach's counterpoint. There is no describing or sufficiently extolling the music. We can realize here, if we never realized before, the fundamental and indispensable basis of the art of structural music that was laid by the supreme Bach and his predecessors and contemporaries of the polyphonic school. These are the beams and arches of the music that was to follow. This gigantic Passacaglia is not only Bach speaking; it is the spirit and the inheritance of his great school, of the labors and dreams of a thousand lesser men, who toiled as humbly and anonymously as the masons who worked, decade after decade, century after century, on Gothic cathedrals. Engrossed in their toil, they were unaware of the greatness of the task, but consecrated to it. They prepared the way—those smaller musicians—for the Master, great and humble, who also labored in obscurity and humility, till the Lord took his sight from him. But his eyes glimpsed the reaches of eternity.

CHRISTOPH WILLIBALD GLUCK

1714–1787

Overture to "Iphigenia in Aulis"

GLUCK'S overture to his opera "Iphigenia in Aulis" ("Iphigenie en Aulide") is a little more than a century and a half old. Unpretentious in its proportions, it is nevertheless one of the greatest of the musical utterances of its time. By means of a noble simplicity and purity of phrase it combines drama and form, passion and repose, in a way that approaches the spirit of Greek tragedy. Wagner described the dramatic motives of the opera, present in the overture, as those of appeal, power, grace and pity. Pathetic dialogue of the strings precedes the stern rhythmic motive which introduces the main movement—the voice of the inexorable gods. The grand flourish of brass and strings, several times repeated, pompous in the manner of the French classic drama (Gluck's subject came to him from the theatre of Racine via the opera libretto of Du Roullet), is like unto the commentary of a Greek chorus.

Wagner considered this overture Gluck's greatest instrumental composition, and there is no good reason to disagree with him. The last measures of the overture led originally into the first act of the opera. Concert endings have been composed by Mozart and Wagner. Wagner's conclusion, most often used, substitutes thirty-three measures of his own for Gluck's transitional passage. These measures are constructed reverently upon phrases already heard, returning to the music of the opening, concluding with the motive of the gods' decree ominously muttering in the basses.

This overture and the work which it preludes were first performed at the Opéra, Paris, April 19, 1774. "Iphigenia in Aulis" was the second of five operas, based on classic themes, in which Gluck wrought immense and much-needed reforms in the fields of music drama. The French operatic stage had become extremely conventionalized, and the attention of the public centred less upon dramatic expression and consistency of style than upon the ballet and the solo dancers, who even superseded the leading singers in popular favor. The famous Vestris, who called himself the god of the ballet, asked Gluck kindly to insert a chaconne for him in the last act. When Gluck exploded, asking Vestris when he ever heard of the Greeks dancing chaconnes, the "god" exclaimed, "Did they not, indeed? Well, then, so much the worse for them!" Gluck, aided by the best minds of the day, and by Marie Antoinette, his former pupil, triumphed over Vestris and his kind. Nor was Paris lacking in appreciation of his genius. The minds that bred the French Revolution were there. Voltaire and Jean-Jacques Rousseau were among Gluck's defenders. When it was made known to the authorities of the Académie Royale de Musique that Gluck had "written a French opera, which he earnestly desires to bring to Paris," the answer was, "If the Chevalier Gluck is willing to pledge himself to write six operas of this kind for the Academy, well and good; otherwise it cannot be played, for such a work as this is calculated to kill all the old French operas." The full text of the reply may be found in Ernest Newman's study of Gluck ("Gluck and the Opera"), from which work the following paragraph, for the better understanding of the music, is well worth quoting:

"Year after year the language of an art grows richer and more complex, and work after work sinks into ever-deepening oblivion; until music that once thrilled men with delirious ecstasy becomes a dead thing which here and there the student looks upon in a mood of scarcely tolerant antiquarianism. In the temple of art a hundred statues of the gods are overthrown; and a hundred others stand with arrested lips and inarticulate tongues, pale symbols of a vanished dominion which men no longer own. Yet here and there through the ghostly twilight comes the sound of some clear voice that has defied the courses of the years and the mutations of taste; and we hear the rich canorous tones of Gluck, not perhaps with all the vigor and the passion that once was theirs, but with the mellowed splendor given by the touch of time. Alone among his fellows he speaks our modern tongue, and chants the eternal passions of the race. He was indeed, as Sophie Arnould called him, 'the musician of the soul'; and if we have added new strings to our lyre, and wrung from them a more poignant eloquence than ever stirred within the heart of Gluck, none the less do we perceive that music such as his comes to us from the days when there were giants in the land."

FRANZ JOSEPH HAYDN

1732–1809

THE enduring structure of the classic symphony was perfected and established for the generations by Haydn. Rubinstein was in the habit of referring condescendingly to "papa Haydn." Von Bülow rejoined: "Yes! But when he is great-grandfather Rubinstein, Haydn will still be 'papa' Haydn!" The conventional view of Haydn is that of a man who was principally a formalist in music, whose feelings did not run deep, who had little contact with life, who was content to pin eighteenth-century patterns of tone, very charming but with little significance beyond the grace and felicity of the musical design.

As a matter of fact, Haydn knew life and knew it at first hand. He lived it with curiosity and gusto, and expressed a vigorous and often imaginative disposition in his music. He was anything but the slavish follower of convention, being in fact a pioneer in his art, always experimenting and reshaping the symphonic form, of which he was the first great and acknowledged master. Into this form he wove fabric of the court and country-side, for he knew both phases of existence. Modern research shows that Haydn was almost certainly not Austrian, but Croatian, which means Slav, by birth. Himself of peasant origin, he was politic, respectful, and at home in the presence of the *haute monde*. He was quick and shrewd enough to estimate accurately the conditions that encompassed him, and make them stepping-stones to honor and frame, but he was neither the insulated musician nor the lackey of nobility that some would make him. He wore a uniform and fulfilled with genius the duties of musical factotum to Prince Esterházy. After all, it wasn't a bad uniform.

Socially speaking, Haydn was fenced off from the nobles whom he served, but he had his own orchestra to work and experiment with, and not one but two theatres equipped for drama, opera or marionette performances. Steadily he grew in his art. His position was the one conventionally assigned to a musician of that day. Sometimes one wonders whether the social insulation of that period, and the hard routine labor to which he was subjected, did not benefit the composer. Today a Stravinsky is dined and wined by our best people. European princesses and American millionaires shower entertainment upon him. In the olden time a Bach or a Haydn was expected to turn out his weekly scores—a quartet, a symphony, a piece of hack music belike—all in the day's work, and no fuss about it. Thus he acquired an immensely fluent and solid technic. When it came to the higher things of life and the thoughts that go to the creation of masterpieces, he was thrown back on himself. He plumbed his own soul and drew from within and not from some outside source the creative power that stood him in such good stead with posterity.//

The industrious composer of the first classic symphonies, quartets, the "Creation" and innumerable other works found life intensely worth living; mingled with the great "nor lost the common touch"; married a Xantippe of a wife, but loved more than one fascinating woman; more than gave value received for the existence with which God had endowed him; and lived to a ripe age, complaining at the last that he was only beginning to know how to compose music.

•

Symphony in D major ("With the Horn Signal")—(B. & H. No. 31)

I. Allegro
II. Adagio
III. Menuet
IV. Finale (Theme with Variations)

In the year of Our Lord 1764 Haydn composed his "symphony with the horn-call." Haydn makes the three movements of the symphony as cultivated by Sammartini four. He also uses, probably

[24]

for the first time in the history of the symphony, four horns in place of the customary two. Haydn found relief from music-making, while retainer of Prince Esterházy, by shooting and fishing on his estate. This symphony is said to echo "the joy of the chase." The horn-call is heard at once, played by all four horns in unison. In a moment the answering call of a solo horn, as from far off, is heard. There were no clarinets in the Haydn symphony. Mozart was to sponsor that instrument. Haydn uses only flutes, oboes, the four horns and the customary strings. In the second movement there are dialogues between the instruments— first a violin solo, then dialogue between solo violin and two horns, then solo 'cello, and the string choir. Haydn was constantly making new experiments in instrumental combinations. The third movement is the customary minuet. The finale is a set of variations.

As you listen to this music you realize in it the taste of another period, and also the slower tempo of an age and environment not that of today. This symphony could never have sprung up in the period of radio, aëroplanes, taxicabs, and noise which the human race packed in the cities incredibly endures. We can envy its adorable beauty, serenity and superfine workmanship!

●

Symphony in E flat major (B. & H. No. 103)

    I.   Adagio; Allegro con spirito
    II. Andante
    III. Menuetto; Trio
    IV. Finale: Allegro con spirito

In his later years Haydn travelled twice to London, where he was lionized and rewarded munificently. Students of his works find the symphonies which he wrote for the London impresario Salomon richer in their content than other compositions that Haydn cast in the same form. This special importance is attributed by them not only to Haydn's maturity as a composer, but to the effect of the new experiences and impressions of his journey, and, very possibly, the fertilizing influence of his contact with the younger Mozart.

The twelve Salomon symphonies were published in two sets of six each. The one here discussed is No. 3 of the second set. It is the so-called "symphony with the kettledrum-roll." In its pages Haydn conducts several experiments, some of them looking to the future of symphonic music. One of these is the reappearance of a theme heard in the introduction in the main movement which follows.

Ordinarily, in Haydn's day, the slow introduction of the first movement of a symphony was a mere ceremonious prelude to what followed. It established atmosphere and gained the attention of the audience.

But in this symphony the portentous theme, preceded by a drum-roll, which stalks about in the opening measures of the introduction, returns, like a spectre at the feast, in the midst of quick and gay music that follows. This occurs towards the end of the movement, after a brilliant passage and a pause, or "fermata." There, again, we hear the drum-roll, followed by the theme in its original form. But Haydn has done subtler things than that. In a later place he gives a fragment of the introductory theme to his violas and 'cellos—following another "fermata"; and the coda, or concluding part of the movement, begins with a phrase of the same introductory theme, so altered in rhythm and form that one must look twice to realize its origin.

The second movement is a theme with variations. The theme has among other distinguishing characteristics the fact that it is half in the major key and half in the minor. The first section is C major, the second C minor. The variations hold to this harmonic scheme. It is not until the coda that Haydn allows his fancy to wander freely through distant keys and tonal vistas that freshly enchant us. Croatian melodies are in this symphony, including the first theme of the first movement proper: the theme on which the variations of the slow movement are built; the chief theme of the last movement.

•

Symphony in C minor (B. & H. No. 95)

I. Allegro moderato
II. Andante cantabile
III. Menuetto
IV. Finale—Vivace

The very popular symphony in C minor is another of the set that Haydn composed for Salomon. At the concerts where this symphony was performed Salomon led the orchestra, standing. Haydn sat at the harpsichord. Not only the composer but Salomon had reason to be gratified with the symphony's reception. The work dispenses with an introduction. The first theme has a virility not unsuggestive of the young Beethoven. This theme is dwelt upon by Haydn; it is extensively manipulated. The closing pages of the movement, which begins in the minor key, are in the major. The second movement is a characteristic theme with variations. The menuetto is well known for the charm of the 'cello solo which makes its middle part, and the finale is unusually vigorous and substantial in workmanship.

THE CLASSIC SYMPHONY

THE classic symphony is an evolution and synthesis of what had been going on in instrumental composition for centuries. It assembled within its walls the technical achievements of centuries of harmony and counterpoint, formal elements of dance and song, and the resource, new in the late eighteenth century, of brilliant and varied instrumental color. For it happened that the orchestra developed coincidentally with the symphony.

The movements were arranged in such succession and proportion as to secure an architectural structure, and within the outlines of that structure richness of content and balance of design.

The perfected symphony of Haydn and Mozart was in four movements, contrasted in form, tempo and key.

The first movement, often preceded by a stately introduction, had customarily a lively pulse, and while other designs were optional, was likely to be cast in "sonata form."

[29]

The second movement, ordinarily the slow movement, had a prevailingly lyrical character, and was usually in the form of the extended song or the sonata movement of abridged character.

As the origin of the slow movement was the song, so was the following movement, the minuet—or scherzo, as it became later—a three-part form derived from forms of the dance.

The finale could take various forms. That of the sonata was frequently employed. Another form was the rondo, which derived its name from the poetical verse with a recurring refrain. Another was the theme and variations. With Haydn the last movement of a symphony had usually the quality of lively entertainment, but with the symphonists from Beethoven on this movement tended to become a dramatic climax or monumental summing up of the entire symphony.

*   *   *

The movement-structure bearing the name "sonata form" is essentially a three-part design, based upon two leading themes, contrasted in character and key. The main divisions, closely linked together, are known as Exposition, Development or Free Fantasia, and Recapitulation. The Exposition publishes the musical material of the movement. In the Development section that material, or any part of it, is freely developed. The Recapitulation is the repetition and often amplification of the material of the Exposition, with

[30]

emphasis of the key of the movement. At the end there is added a concluding passage, known as the "coda."

The first theme of the sonata movement is likely to be the more energetic of its two leading motives, and the second to be more lyrical in character. As the symphony develops, these themes are the more significantly contrasted. The entrance of the second theme is in most cases carefully prepared. Between the two principal themes is musical connective tissue in the form of passage-work, or even a sub-theme of accessory character. After the second theme comes further material designed to round out the Exposition. It may be an extension of motives already heard, or fresh passage-work, or other subsidiary matter. By some this completion of the Exposition is called the "codetta"—that is, the "little coda"—anticipating in its purpose the greater coda that comes at the end of the movement.

Generally, in order to impress this material on the listener, and give added definition to the movement, the Exposition is repeated before the composer proceeds to the Development. There he manipulates his themes and modulates into such keys as he pleases. This part of the movement gives him special opportunity for original procedure, always keeping in mind that he must stick to his ideas, develop them with skill and interest, and return in a logical and interesting way to his initial theme, in its original form, for the

[31]

Recapitulation. The principal difference between the Recapitulation and Exposition is the fact that both the principal themes, originally stated in different keys, are now restated in the basic key of the movement; that the connecting passages between the themes are altered in their progress with this end in view; and finally, that to the customarily amplified material of the Exposition is added the coda, as completion of the composer's thought.

The details of the other movements of the symphony can best be exemplified by describing them as they actually occur in a work which is a supreme model of classic beauty, Mozart's symphony in G minor.

WOLFGANG AMADEUS MOZART ·

1756–1791

Symphony in G minor (Köchel, 550)

I. Allegro molto
II. Andante
III. Menuetto: Allegro
IV. Allegro assai

A CROWNING marvel of this symphony is its seraphic union of form and feeling. This perfection, transparency and grace can even deceive us as to the passionate import of the music. The agitation and forboding of the opening movement give place to the mystical tenderness and seraphic melancholy of the Andante. The Menuetto, formal as it is, and set in strict designs of the dance, has nevertheless a special energy, and the lovely middle part is the lovelier for the contrast. The last movement, beginning with a figure familiar enough in Mozart's day, develops with a wholly exceptional brilliancy and dramatic fire. The profundity of Mozart's music is embodied in the apparent simplicity of its style.

The G minor symphony has no introduction. The agitated first theme (1) is played by the violins. The connecting episode begins twenty-eight measures later (2), with bold accents of the full orchestra, and

[33]

leaps of the strings, followed by rushing scale figures. Two sharp chords, followed by a short pause, prepare the entrance of the second theme (3).

The first theme was in G minor, the basic key of the symphony. The second is in the key of B flat, known as the "relative major." This melody is of an entirely different nature from the first, and is colored differently by the instruments, the strings alternating with wind instruments in its statement. Brilliant figures and reminiscences of the first theme make the "codetta" (4) and bring the Exposition to an end.

The Exposition is now repeated, but this time its finishing chords, with an abrupt change of key, switch us into the Development section (5), which is devoted entirely to the dramatic treatment of the first theme. These opposed elements contest, as it were, for the mastery, until, with sighing dialogue of strings and wind, a most adroit and graceful return is made to the first theme in its original form, and we are arrived at the Recapitulation (6).

This Recapitulation follows strictly the dictates of the Form. The material of the Exposition is repeated and filled out somewhat. The second theme (7) appears now in the same key as the first, and with some extension of the episodic matter. To the material of the Recapitulation is added the dramatic coda (8), which is short, very poignant and expressive, and based, in turn, upon the same agitated theme which has preoccupied the composer through the course of the whole movement. 280902

The Andante is composed in the "abridged sonata form." In this variant of the form there are first (9) and second (10) themes, but they are not so strongly contrasted as in the complete sonata movement and they dispense with connecting episodes. In fact, this movement of Mozart partakes of the natures of both the sonata and the elaborated song form which often makes the second part of the symphony. That form consists in a first division of sustained melody, then a more animated contrasting passage, and thereafter a return to the melody of the first part. The principal difference between the song form and the "abridged sonata" design exists in the fact that in the latter instance the contrasting part is genuine Development (11) of themes previously heard, instead of new contrasting material; and so it is in the slow movement of this symphony, which gives the impression of one central thought, expanded and developed by the composer.

The Menuetto in dance rhythms is in three-part form, with each section subdivided into three smaller parts. It is thus a succession of dance figures, so arranged and developed as to effectively balance each other. The divisions and sub-divisions are readily recognizable. The first part announces an energetic motive (12), a few bars in length, then develops it (13), then returns to the initial idea (14) in variation

[35]

and with a codetta. The second part follows the same tripartite design, distinguished by a first (15) motive, a second (16), and a return to the first (17). Thereafter comes the repetition of the first part which completes the movement.

The last movement opens with a theme (18) cast in the intervals of a simple chord leaping upward, arpeggio-fashion. The theme is repeated. Then comes the customary (19) episode, and later the same preparation as in the opening movement for the second theme (20). Its song is given the first violins over the accompaniment of second violins and violas. After repetition and extension by progressions for the wind instruments the development section (21) starts with brusque announcement in unison, by all the instruments except the horns, of a variation of the first phrase of the "rocket" subject. [The ascending arpeggio figure, used by many composers of the period, as also by Beethoven, came to be known as the "Mannheim rocket".] The Recapitulation (22), led into by a version of the theme in the bass, brings the movement to an end.

MENUETTO
Allegro

FINALE

Allegro assai

Symphony in E flat (Köchel 543)

I. Adagio; Allegro
II. Andante
III. Menuetto: Allegretto
IV. Finale: Allegro

This is the first of the three symphonies in E flat, G minor, and C major which Mozart finished, within less than six weeks' time, in the year 1788. That was a year of misfortune and of gigantic creation. Each of the three masterpieces referred to has distinctive qualities which put it apart from the others. The symphony in E flat takes a special position, due in the first place to its inherent worth, and in the second to the fact that it is a link of exceptional significance between Mozart and Beethoven. It prophesies nothing less than the towering "Eroica."

It is altogether probable that Beethoven was familiar with this work of Mozart's, and that he had given it careful study before he composed the third of his nine compositions in the same form. Whether or not that is the case, we have here a remarkable example of the manner in which one great master springs from and builds upon the achievement of the other.

The first movement of Mozart's E flat symphony is identic not only in key but in the rhythm, unusual for an opening symphonic movement of that day, of 3-4, with the first part of the "Eroica." There are close relations not only of themes but of harmonies. The harsh dissonance which makes a famous feature

[43]

of the first movement of the "Eroica"—the E set shrilly against the F, as see a later chapter—is present in the same chord, though in a different key, in measure eighteen of Mozart's introduction. The first theme of the "Eroica" had already been anticipated by the eleven-year old Mozart in his operetta, "Sebastien et Sebastienne." But if measures twenty-nine to thirty-two of the allegro of Mozart's first movement are examined, there will be found, note for note, with only slight difference of accent, Beethoven's transformation of his opening theme in the scherzo of the "Eroica." Going farther along in Mozart's score, one finds in measures sixty-four to seventy, large as life, the quick energetic rhythmic figuration that Beethoven uses as episodic material in the "Eroica's" corresponding movement.

It should be added that the E-flat symphony of Mozart stands in no need of the references to Beethoven to proclaim its greatness. The opening movement has a magnificent substance and concision. The richness and depth of melodic expression in the next movement are such as Haydn at his richest could hardly attain. The brilliant Menuetto, which with its gallant pulse and swing can well suggest a blazing ball-room of Mozart's time, is one of the most popular movements he ever composed. The sparkling finale has the humor and the touches of adroit and amusing instrumentation that come straight from Haydn, whom Mozart held in such gratitude and esteem.

Symphony in C major ("Jupiter")
(Köchel, 551)

I. Allegro vivace
II. Andante cantabile
III. Menuetto: Allegretto
IV. Finale: Molto allegro

The "Jupiter" symphony, said by some to derive its nickname from the Jovian energy of its opening thunder-rolls, is the exultant antithesis of the passion and tragedy of the incomparable G minor. "There are things in the world," said Schumann, "about which nothing can be said, as Mozart's C major symphony with the fugue, much of Shakespeare, and pages of Beethoven." Mark the qualifications of Shakespeare and Beethoven, and the unconditional adoration of Mozart. Each movement of the "Jupiter" symphony is a powerful and surpassing creation.

The capstone of this towering symphony is of course the fugue-finale, wherein the polyphonic workmanship of the old fugue is used, with other material, for the perfect consummation of the composer's thought, and the eternal glory of art. The movement is based on an ecclesiastical motive which Mozart employed several times, and which has been used by many composers, from Bach to Arthur Sullivan. This theme, on Mozart's wings, promptly leaves the earth and soars on a dizzying flight to the skies. The finale is made wholly of pure spirit. The complexities of the development only enrich and make the more sunny and glorious the music. There is indeed no match for this movement in the literature of the symphony. There are other compositions—a few equal to it in interest, but there are no others like it, even in Mozart. That is his symphonic apotheosis— the fugue-finale of the "Jupiter" symphony.

Then, when a Mozart who was merely an immortal master had provided an aristocratic company of his day with such food of the gods for their delectation, he could go out and eat with the rest of the servants. If anyone thinks that Mozart enjoyed these social experiences, he has only to read letters of the miraculous artist whom the Archbishop of Salzburg had kicked from his palace, whom an emperor underpaid and insulted, who died young, whose body was cast into an unknown grave, and to whom the world has ever since paid homage. "The composer of 'Don Giovanni' and the 'Jupiter' symphony," as Mr. Philip Hale has remarked, "was unfortunate in his emperors." Mozart's miserable lot would have been intolerable to him if he had not possessed the consolation of his genius. But how he suffered! The more for the fact that his senses were keen, the love of life strong within him, and his spirit greater than his frame. He paid that much to create heavenly music.

LUDWIG VAN BEETHOVEN

1770–1827

Symphony No. 1, in C major, Opus 21

   I.   Adagio molto; Allegro con brio
  II.   Andante cantabile con moto
 III. Menuetto: Allegro molto e vivace; Trio
 IV. Finale: Adagio; Allegro molto e vivace

ON THE second of April, 1800, Ludwig van Beethoven, then thirty years old, and eight years in Vienna, where he had come to study composition with
Haydn, announced a benefit concert, with a program
which would include "A new grand symphony for
full orchestra by Beethoven." On the same program
was also a symphony "by the late chapel-master Mozart; an aria and duet from Haydn's 'Creation' ";
also "a grand concerto for pianoforte, played and
composed by Beethoven," and "a septet for four
strings and three wind instruments, composed by
Beethoven." Tickets and stalls were to be had of
"Herr van Beethoven at his lodgings im tiefen
Graben, No. 241, third story, and of the box-keeper."
There is no record of speculators selling tickets on the
streets, or of disappointed throngs being turned away
by the "box-keeper." The men in the orchestra
thought the music difficult. The critic of the "All-

gemeine Musikalisches Zeitung" was favorably impressed by the ideas, but thought the wind instruments "used far too much, so that the music is more like a band than an orchestra." When the symphony was performed at Leipzig in November of the following year it was referred to as "the confused explosions of the outrageous effrontery of a young man." In Paris, as late as 1810, it was written that the "astonishing success" of Beethoven's music was "a danger to the musical art. . . . It is believed that a prodigal use of the most barbaric dissonances and a noisy use of all the orchestral instruments will make an effect. Alas, the ear is only stabbed; there is no appeal to the heart."

This of Beethoven's First symphony! Listen to it, this work cited in the 1800's to prove Beethoven "a danger to the musical art."

Beethoven is trying, in this first symphony of his, to respect the forms and standards of earlier masters than himself, particularly Haydn and Mozart. He is a little constrained in their mold, and occasionally cannot help revealing the cloven hoof of the revolutionist beneath the gown of the respectful disciple. But it is a delightful symphony, and a model of inspiration balanced by control and self-sacrifice. Beethoven was willing to bide his time and learn his business. The melodic clarity of this work is enhanced by its conciseness, concentration and complete absence of superfluities. The themes themselves are reduced to the shortest number of notes consistent with the meat of the idea. The energy of the first movement is well balanced by the gracefulness of the slow movement that follows. The dignified minuet of the Mozart period has become quickened and energized. There is a charming conceit in the introduction of the finale— in the hesitation with which the violins unfold the introductory phrase, like a cat approaching cream, and this finale has much of Haydn's humor and bustle. But it is Beethoven who speaks.

●

Symphony No. 2, in D major, Opus 36

I.   Adagio molto; Allegro con brio
II. Larghetto
III. Scherzo: Allegro
IV. Finale: Allegro molto

Beethoven's Second symphony was composed in the years 1801 and 1802, those years when nature pronounced upon the composer the sentence of complete deafness; when he knew the terror of the silence inexorably closing upon him; when his love for the youthful Countess Giulietta Guicciardi, though returned, was pronounced hopeless so far as marriage was concerned, and when, in the summer of 1802, hiding from men, Beethoven flung on paper that cry of loneliness and agony, found after his death, which is known as "Heiligenstadt Will."

[49]

Camille Bellaigne called the work "a heroic lie," for the mood of the symphony is one of strength and joy—Beethoven confronting life and proudly aware of the power of his genius. Between his First and Second symphonies, while there is no such gap as that which separates the Second and Third, there is a distance eloquent of interior growth. The Second symphony is intensified and expanded Mozart, but Mozart on ampler lines, and impregnated with a new force. The introduction alone would be notice of a new figure in music. It is Beethoven's salute to the life and beauty of the world. The unison opening has a force and simplicity that he never lost. Little by little, rhythm and melody accumulate. The orchestra gradually brightens, glowing with new colors, as a valley between mountains takes upon itself splendor upon splendor with the sunrise.

The main movement, bold and gay, begins with a waggish theme that creeps along in the lower strings until suddenly it explodes with the full force of the orchestra. Beethoven takes a bit of this theme and from it makes much of the movement. The singing second theme is played by wind instruments over the accompaniment of the strings and answered jubilantly by the tutti. Between these themes are flashing episodes, but most of the movement rests upon the jester's quip of five notes—a nugget so small that few composers but Beethoven would have seen anything in it.

The slow movement is devoted principally to a lovely melody, relieved by some lighter byplay, which also is a lineal descendant of Mozart. There is little more graceful and felicitous in music of the classic period than this movement, yet it is a fact that Beethoven revised it many times. A smaller man might have gone stale through such polishing, but the longer Beethoven labored on a composition, the more concise, natural and eloquent it became.

The scherzo, with its "spirit and vigor . . . almost seems to fly at your throat"—the words are Sir George Grove's. Here are abrupt alternations of soft and loud, sudden changes of key and contrasts of instrumentation—guffaws and disturbances which must have given in the early 1800's the impression of a particularly lively and impish bull in a china shop! And in these two last movements appears a device destined to come later into more general use, of repeating thematic ideas in different movements. If one listens attentively to the first part of the scherzo as it flashes by, he will notice that the five-note figure of the first movement returns, to be inserted with a surprising neatness and deftness in the tonal design.

The finale, full of pranks and harlequinade, begins with a clown's somersault from the high to the low register of the first violins. A transplantation of material from the first movement comes with the repetition of an episode of that movement, played by certain of the lower instruments in unison, and disappearing almost as quickly as it raised its head in the orchestra. The diverting effect of the transplantations here and in the scherzo is increased by their air of byplay and innocence—as if Beethoven just chanced to think of the business as the music whizzed by.

And here, with this work, we have the complete foundation of the symphonic orchestra, with its three complete choirs and the kettledrums, the principal element in the "battery" of percussion instruments that developed later. The string choir consists of the first and second violins, the violas, violoncellos—'cellos for short—and double-basses. The woodwind division comprises flutes, oboes, clarinets and bassoons. The horns and trumpets of the brass choir have yet to be augmented by the trombones that came with Beethoven's Fifth symphony, and by the tubas and other wind instruments that Berlioz and Wagner added. But here is the symphonic nucleus—and note Beethoven's orchestration. Already he has found a way of his own of using the instruments. They have in his hands a special vibrancy and power. These clear, flashing colors and explosions of force will from now on be characteristic of his orchestral style.

"But why," says Grove, "talk of 'parts and movements'? Who has time to think of them while his ears are full of such delicious sound? Even now [Grove writes in the Eighteen Eighties] what can be newer or pleasanter to hear than the whole symphony? To this very day, eighty years after its first appearance, the whole work is as fresh as ever in its indomitable fiery flash and its irresistible strength. Were ever fiddles more brilliant, more rampant in their freaks and vagaries, bursting out like flames in the pauses of the wind, exulting in their strength and beauty, than they are here? . . . Had ever the bassoon and oboe such parts before?—and so on throughout. No one has beaten it, not even Beethoven himself. Listen to it and see if we are not right."

Grove's words hold true. Beethoven was to write greater symphonies than the Second. But this early work has a place of its own, which cannot be usurped, among the Nine.

●

Symphony No. 3, in E flat major ("Eroica"), Opus 55

I.   Allegro con brio
II. Marcia funebre: Adagio assai
III. Scherzo: Allegro vivace; Trio
IV. Finale: Allegro molto

The inspiration of the "Eroica" symphony, and the manner in which Beethoven changed its dedication, are strangely symbolic of the nature of the composition and the place that it occupies in art. We know that when Beethoven began this symphony he had in mind Napoleon Bonaparte. There is no question about this. The erased dedication on the manuscript title-page of the symphony is the evidence. But when Beethoven thought of Napoleon he thought of the First Consul of the new French Republic, the liberator of humanity, the destroyer of kingcraft and all that that estate implied. Then Beethoven received the news that Napoleon had had himself declared Emperor. He tore up the dedication page in fury, crying out that Napoleon had become nothing but an ordinary man, "and now he will turn tyrant." And the symphony was described on the title-page as "composed to celebrate the memory of a great man." The work, in other words, was re-dedicated, not to Napoleon, the cracked statue of a hero, but to the heroic spirit in man. *That* became Beethoven's theme. *That* was what Bonaparte stood for in Beethoven's mind when he composed the symphony. And so we have a score cleansed, as it were, of any literal or programmatic associations, which treats not of an individual but of an ideal, in terms of the greatest music. There is no attempt here to give us a portrait of the dress and the buttons of a hero, or the deeds of an egotistical individual—anything but such an attempt as Richard Strauss made when he celebrated himself in his tone-poem "Ein Heldenleben" ("A Hero's Life"). The "Eroica," or "heroic," symphony is impersonal as the tomb of the Unknown Soldier, a monument to the deathless spirit of man. It is as if a mysterious destiny, in causing Beethoven agony by tearing down an idol before his

eyes, had taken the ultimate pains to insure the greatest destiny for his creation. We have in this work not
a personal outpouring so much as a masterpiece which
balances form and profound feeling, and looks down
from its height on the music of two centuries.

Therefore, there is no program for this symphony
such as Beethoven gave us for the "Pastorale." But
the thought back of the work is obvious in the musical material. The gap in style between this symphony
of Beethoven—his Third—and the Second symphony,
which it followed by an interval of only one year, is
deep and wide. There is perhaps no greater leap in
the symphonic evolution of any composer. The distance between the works has been explained as due to
development in other scores, not symphonies, which
came from Beethoven's pen in the intervening period. But I cannot find in those other scores any real
approach to the "Eroica." The real cause of the
change is the impregnation of Beethoven's thought by
a new intellectual conception.

The first movement of the symphony is surely to
be construed as the picture, in broadest and most impersonal terms, of heroic character, in which resolve
and tenderness, faith and the tragic consciousness,
have equal representation. There is no formal introduction, as there was in the earlier symphonies of
Beethoven—merely two brusque major chords and
the immediate announcement of the hero theme. It is
a theme bare to starkness, very plain, and based on

[55]

intervals of the commonest chord. It is announced and expanded by the orchestra. Between this theme and the second are long connecting passages which are no longer episodes or mere connecting passage works, but significant musical ideas, closely related to and expansive of the import of the main themes. The architecture of the movement is on the grandest lines. The second theme is less a melody than a succession of chords—in other words, a *harmonic* rather than a *melodic* theme, tender and lofty in sentiment. It is noticeable that in this symphony, unlike the works of Beethoven's predecessors, there is not the sharp demarcation and partitioning off of first from second and subsidiary themes. The movement is much more plastic and connected in its parts—more so than any earlier symphony Beethoven had written. The treatment of the ideas is lengthy, and very rich and bold. The hero theme is endlessly manipulated, and always with fresh resource. In one place, after the exposition of his material, Beethoven drives home repeated sharp dissonances—chords in which an "E natural" rasps against an "F"—with the most startling and dramatic effect. The place is thrown into higher relief by the suave harmonies which immediately follow.

All this and much more takes place in the first two-thirds of the first movement of the symphony, which comprises the Exposition of the themes and their free development. The return to the Recapitulation of the material of the Exposition is accomplished in such an individual manner as to have disconcerted Beethoven's contemporaries. In fact, Beethoven's pupil Ries, at the first rehearsal, thought that this intentionally dissonant passage was a mistake in the score, and nearly got his ears boxed for calling the composer's attention to it. The passage is the one in which the solo horn, playing the first notes of the hero themes, appears to come in too soon, against a harmony that does not belong to it. Two measures later the horn repeats its motive, now with the right harmony, and we have the long and splendid repetition of the Exposition and the "coda," or peroration of the movement. This movement in itself is almost a symphony.

Its antithesis is the epic lamentation of the second movement, the incommensurable Funeral March. It is said that after he had eradicated Napoleon's name from his score, Beethoven never again referred to him, until he was told, seventeen years later, of Napoleon's death at St. Helena. He is reported to have said, "I have already composed the proper music for the catastrophe." If he said that, he underestimated his dirge, which is for all humanity. The march begins heavily, tragically, in the minor key. Later, in the middle part, it changes to major, with a more sustained and consoling song. But the emotional climax is reached by means of a fugal development (Measure 114) followed by the awful proclamations of the trombones which made Theodore Thomas think of the Resurrection Day—and that does not exaggerate the tragic grandeur of the passage. You will notice the touch of drama and spectacle at the end of the march —the broken, disjointed fragments of the march, played softly, with pauses of silence between the fragments, as if the last words of leave-taking and homage had been choked by sobs.

Many, Thomas among them, find in these first two movements of the symphony the real "Eroica," rating them as distinct, apart from and superior to the movements which follow. Others, making no unfavorable comparisons, are puzzled to discover the relation between the two first and the two last themes, especially as the movements which make the second half of the symphony are joyous in tone. How are they to be construed? The scherzo is music of joyous rustlings and horn-calls; it has the tang of the Autumn forest, and the promise of Nature's eternal cycle of deaths and resurrections. The finale, the capstone of the gigantic creation, is a set of variations on a simple, stark theme.

Each listener will have his own explanation of these movements. For some the scherzo will be the voice of what we know as life, murmuring strangely and joyously of the glory of death. The choice, for the finale, of the theme with the enigmatic repeated B flats, is the highest wisdom, a theme that grew for years in Beethoven's consciousness. He had used it first, in a com-

paratively superficial way, in his "Prometheus" ballet;
then as a basis for the fifteen piano variations, Op. 35.
But still he had not plumbed all the secrets of that simple motive. He expands it now on lines that stretch out
into infinity. It is not romantic feeling that Beethoven
seeks here, but something more vast and eternal. He
has done with transient emotions, profound as they
may be, and immortalized by him in the first part of
the symphony. That first part was life; this is beyond
life. We have a protean set of variations, pure music,
symbol of order, power, spirit; play of invisible tones
about a certain central point; sovereign evocation of
form and rhythm. Their development includes the
return of the first theme of the symphony, which has
already reappeared, in different disguises, in the Funeral March and the scherzo. Perhaps this finale is the
most "absolute" tonal design to be found in the nine
symphonies. Perhaps, because of its balance of emotion and thought, feeling and form, and all-surpass-
ing grandeur of design, the "Eroica" will one day
stand forth as the greatest of all symphonies.

●

Symphony No. 4, in B flat major, Opus 60

I. Adagio; Allegro vivace
II. Adagio
III. Allegro vivace
IV. Finale: Allegro ma non troppo

Beethoven's Fourth symphony is the point of repose between the immensities of the Third and the Fifth. For this reason it has received less than its just measure of appreciation. Here is no vast dream or troubling self-examination, no effort to storm the heavens or predicate the destiny of man. Beethoven was well content for the moment to forget everything but sun and sky. His orchestra is capable, as that of no other composer, of mirroring the clearness of the atmosphere, which seems to be the source from which this music springs. Perhaps the most original parts of the symphony are the introduction of the first movement and the slow movement. But the word "originality" is one to be used with a certain degree of caution. A composer may invent a new and original chord and say very little. Another composer may take a familiar musical formula and say original things. It is not only the delicious vagueness and suspense of the introduction of this symphony which are original; it is the sudden precipitation of force with which the movement proper leaps from the preceding measures. That is Beethoven, even though the general style of the remainder of the movement is closely related to Haydn. It seems to be natural and inevitable that in this place Beethoven should allow Haydn to be his guide, but it is Haydn surcharged with the greater virility of his successor. The slow movement is as if nature stood on tiptoe, her finger to her lips. It is one of many slow movements Beethoven composed in which the music goes past thought, past books, men, or cities. These tell about creation, but Beethoven's music is part of it.

●

Symphony No. 5, in C minor, Opus 67

I. Allegro con brio
II. Andante con moto
III. Scherzo
IV. Finale

It was Robert Schumann who said that revolution might be confined within the four walls of a symphony and the police be none the wiser. Beethoven's revolution is inaugurated with the famous motive of four notes (1), of which he is supposed to have said "Thus fate knocks at the door." It has never been proved that Beethoven originated this phrase, but it expresses the music. Those four notes, those imperious knocks of destiny on the door, proclaim a new spirit and a new day. Nothing could be simpler, and more blunt, imperious, unsafe for the established order. With that roar of rage Beethoven strides upon the scene, and his mien is terrible. I think of a

[61]

poem, in which the aristocrats of Louis's court are at pretty play, dressed as shepherds and shepherdesses, behind high stone walls. Suddenly a head, dishevelled, hideous, leers over the wall. There is a pause of consternation, till the head, with a horrible laugh, disappears, herald of violence and destruction for those who thought themselves safe forever behind their walls. Beethoven's four-note motive, which must have sounded appallingly in select symphonic circles of Europe, is like that head—prophet of war!

Observe what happens after those four notes, loaded with dynamite, have been twice sounded. How these same notes, with their savage and implacable force, invest the orchestra! Observe this too: Beethoven's practical abnegation of melodic forms, phrases, or periods, in favor of rhythm. Here is almost nothing but the onslaught of rhythm which sweeps everything before it (2). There is a moment of brief melody —the second theme (3), introduced by a powerful variant of the first—melody which hangs like a flower over the abyss, while the obstinate rhythm threatens underneath—melody which is swept away like everything else so unfortunate as to be in the path of this Vesuvian eruption! All is shattered, reassembled, and shattered again by the driving power of the rhythm. Perhaps you will notice a place about two-thirds through the first movement, when chords are exchanged softly by different instruments—strings and woodwind—like the sighs of one utterly spent by the conflict, only to be answered with redoubled fury by the whole orchestra. Thus the first movement of Beethoven's Fifth symphony, one of the shortest and the most dramatic he ever composed, is made from the four notes which, if you heard them apart from their context, you would imagine could be invented by any child with one finger on the piano. The structure reared on those four basic tones is one of the proudest that Beethoven achieved.

The second movement of the symphony is in the form of a noble theme, with simple but most eloquent variations. The next two movements are joined, and their dramatic significance is plain from the re-entrance, in varied form, of the Fate theme. Nothing that Beethoven did is more indicative of his manner of turning a classic form to individual purpose than his procedure in the third movement of the Fifth symphony. It is much less a dance than it is a mysterious and catastrophic preparation for the finale, and this preparation hinges on the Fate theme. The opening measures are charged with suspense (4). Basses and 'celli grope about, as if in a troubled dream. When will the sleeper awake? Suddenly a horn raps out the Fate motive in an altered guise (5), but unmistakable in its derivation from the four-note motive of the first movement. Replying to the horn, other instruments take up the theme, chanting it in different choirs. The double-basses, with a rough and energetic motive, gambol clumsily about like the rumblings of an earthquake in the orchestra (6). Signs and portents accumulate. The first part of the scherzo returns in a way which enhances the mystery—almost inaudible pluckings of the strings, whispers of the Fate theme (7), as of something impending, something immense and awful gestating. The orchestra becomes more vague and uncertain—this orchestra of Beethoven's, which has been dealing its sledge-hammer blows at fate. At last it lies supine, like a monster asleep. A single opaque chord is suspended in the atmosphere. Everything is in a mist. Then the drum begins to beat (8), at first very softly, then with an immense crescendo (9) which launches into the triumphant finale.

Symphony No. 6, in F major ("Pastoral"), Opus 68

I. Cheerful impressions awakened by arrival in the country (Allegro ma non troppo)
II. Scene by the brook (Andante molto moto)
III. Merry gathering of country-folk (Allegro)
IV. Thunderstorm—tempest (Allegro)
V. Shepherds' song; glad and grateful feelings after the storm (Allegretto)

There is often occasion to marvel at the fidelity and sensitiveness with which music, mirror of the human spirit, is affected by the slightest breath of feeling or sensation that passes over its surface, and records with a truthfulness beyond the composer's control the deepest secrets of his being. Beethoven calls his Sixth symphony "Pastoral," which, indeed, it is. We would associate it with the country-side without any title. But I think all Beethoven's music of nature is the music of a man who never knew the sea. Only once in his life, as a boy of eleven, did he see the gray and tossing waters. Had he known them, as Wagner and Weber did, we would have had other music from him. But not greater music. The environment of a great spirit cannot constitute a limitation. Beethoven, in the geographical sense, lived in a restricted radius, principally that of Vienna and the beautiful surrounding country. It was from within and not from without that his music came. Had he lived in a prison cell, his vast spirit would have brooded gigantic over the universe. He needed of nature, in the words of Vincent d'Indy, no more than a little nook in a valley, a meadow, a tree. "So it must have been," says d'Indy, "within the narrow limits of some eight or ten miles either to the north of Vienna, or at Baden or Hetzendorf, that there were conceived and written (or at least sketched) not a single 'Pastoral' symphony but ten 'Pastoral' symphonies—that is to say, ten great works, at the fewest, telling of Beethoven's impressions face to face with nature." In the valley of Wildgrube is the path known today as the "Beethovengang" (Beethoven path), which leads to the brook of the "Pastoral" symphony, "the placid and shady Schreiberbach."

Beethoven listened to the monotonous sounds that rose from the fields, the murmur of the brook, the voices of birds and insects, and worshipped. He heard the voice of God in the thunder; he was drunk with the perfume exhaled from drenched earth, plant and flower. The "Pastoral" symphony is a hymn to Nature. It is also program music, arrant program music, although purists and opponents of this method of musical composition attempt to make light of the fact, and to palliate Beethoven's incidental approaches to realism by repeating his oft-quoted words, "More an expression of feeling than portraiture." The fact of a program, as Beethoven showed, is not the least guarantee for or against great music.

Beethoven's descriptive notes for this symphony,

published in the program of the first performance in Vienna, December 22, 1808, are fuller than those now printed in the published score. There are actually five movements in this work, but the last three are joined together, making only three separate movements. The first movement is intended to portray the "Pleasant feelings which awake in man on arriving in the country." The second is the "Scene by the brook." The third movement, or its component—in Beethoven's word, "Piece"—depicts the "Jovial assemblage of country-folk; interrupted by Fourth Piece—Thunder and Storm; to which succeeds Fifth Piece—Beneficent feelings, associated with gratitude to the Godhead after the Storm."

It is said that Beethoven drew to a certain extent upon folksongs of the country-side for this symphony, but it is easier to make the claim than to prove it, although had he done so he would not have lessened the originality of the work. For it is not only the original theme that counts, but the shaping of the theme, the manner in which the mighty blacksmith, Beethoven, pounds and welds his stubborn material into the proper shape to make the framework of the symphony. And it is not only the shaping but the development of the germinal phrases that makes the strength and glory of the great structure. The method adopted by Beethoven in his first movement, designed to portray the happy man's impressions of the country-side, is a special one, bordering on impressionism.

He is deliberately monotonous. There are the stirrings of the idle breeze, the sounds of birds and insects, vague distant calls, absence of emotions or introspections of an individual. In the first movement one little pastoral motive is repeated for fifty-two measures, and it fascinates us. In the second movement the quiet and meaningless murmur of the brook gives us the respiration felt through all the themes and harmonies built upon it. These include the passages in which a flute impersonates the nightingale, an oboe the quail, a clarinet the cuckoo—quasi-humorous details of the tonal picture. In the next part there is typical Beethoven humor in the dance played for the country-folk by some third-rate village band, which strikes the measure, while a bassoonist, who evidently is able to produce only four notes on his antique instrument, brings them in when he can, with an inspired lumpishness which jibes with the other parts! The dance has its middle part, more rude, vigorous, wooden-shoed— the dances in the wood were ruder than those at the inn of the "Zwei Raben," frequented by Beethoven. When the first part of this scherzo returns it is interrupted by the patter of raindrops, and presently the thunderstorm bursts in its fury. M. d'Indy calls attention to Beethoven's scheme of tonality in this symphony. All the movements except this one are in the major. The darker tonality of F minor is reserved for the storm. One hears the thunder and of course the wind. One almost *sees*, with sudden sharp chords of the orchestra, flashes of lightning. The storm departs in the distance, the pipes of shepherds and thankful songs echo through the orchestra. The strings weave beautiful elaborations on these motives, and so the "Pastoral" symphony comes to an end.

•

Symphony No. 7, in A major, Opus 92

I. Poco sostenuto; Vivace
II. Allegretto
III. Presto; Presto meno assai
IV. Finale: Allegro con brio

In contradistinction to the Sixth or "Pastoral" symphony, Beethoven's Seventh has no "program" or dramatic idea back of it. It is purest beauty, and in its impersonality is a hasty retreat from the programmatic indications of the former work. Unfortunately for the effect on lesser minds, Richard Wagner, in writing of the Seventh symphony, called it "the apotheosis of the dance," and his remark, wholly justified in spirit and never intended literally, had dire consequences. The day came when Isidora Duncan "danced" the Seventh symphony. But the work has survived this *bourgeoiserie* and even the gratuitous explanations of commentators who have sought to provide clues to its meaning.

There are none. The Seventh symphony is beyond explanation. The listener is thrilled by the beauty and

[71]

glory of the music. As he gains familiarity with the work, its details become always more distinct and impressive. But see ever so far, the mystery of the music is farther than that. The product of the genius of a man, it becomes mirror of the genius of the universe.

It happens that four of Beethoven's nine symphonies have introductions: the First, Second, Fourth and Seventh. Of these the introduction to the Seventh symphony is the freest in its fantasy, the noblest and most imposing: a majestic chord of the orchestra, a broad, swinging phrase, heard first from the oboe, then strengthened by other instruments as stronger sonorities are needed to chant it against an upward dancing procession of the strings. Other contributory ideas and surprising modulations lead with inevitability to the rhythm of the main body of the movement, established by an oft-repeated E that rings through the air.

On the basis of this rhythm, and the theme that it generates, Beethoven creates virtually his entire main movement. Phrases which are actually parts of the principal idea could be detached and called "second theme" and "sub-theme" to satisfy the analysts; actually there is one theme, one intoxicating idea which Beethoven refuses to leave, and with which he makes marvelous diversion. Certain novelists have told us that when they created a real character, that character seemed to get out of hand, to act of its own initiative, and do things that its creator had not intended. Beethoven's motive appears to have a like individuality and dynamism. Actually it is never beyond control. The composer remains the unquestioned master of his inspiration. The exuberance and abundance of the music show that he could have continued his movement for many more pages than he does, but his sense of proportion is inexorable. There is not a superfluous note in all this plenty. Near the end of the movement comes a celebrated passage which caused another composer—the youthful Weber, whose years had not bestowed enough insight to save him from ridicule for the statement by posterity—to remark that Beethoven was now "quite ripe for the madhouse." It is the great place toward the end where the violoncellos and double-basses, deep down in the orchestra, concern themselves with a powerful, chained bass of five notes which they keep repeating, while overhead a tremendous climax accumulates.

The second movement is the famous "Allegretto." Beethoven originally marked this movement "andante"—slow. He later, and properly, designated more accurately the tempo he wanted as "allegretto" —somewhat fast, or less than fast. The Seventh symphony is without a slow movement. Its mood is too exuberant. It is too free of our planet! Shall this symphony only walk? The main motive of the allegretto is a hymn-like melody—less a melody, perhaps, than a pulse which beats joyfully and persistently in one or another part of the orchestra. The motive is hymned

[73]

by lower strings. Then it is heard combined with a yearning phrase of violas and 'celli. These two figures interweave. Later there is a change from minor to major, and a new melody, in a different rhythm, for clarinets and bassoons. (But even here can be felt in the depths of the orchestra, as if at the base of creation, the unchanging pulse.) When the first subject returns it is treated in a new way, in the fugal manner. A counter-subject in short notes is set against the initial motive. What the composer is driving at is not at first clear, until the hymning theme, with brilliant counterpoint twining about it, is proclaimed by the full orchestra. For a conclusion, fragments of the motive are tossed from instrument to instrument, and the orchestra sounds the same chord which opened the movement, and a rapturous sigh of the violins brings an end.

The third movement, the scherzo, is energized Haydn. This, at least, is true of the first part, a peasant strain. The contrasting passage is one of the supreme moments in Beethoven. The melody here given the strings is said to be that of a pilgrim hymn heard by the master at Teplitz. What gives the passage its singular and haunting beauty is the A, preceded by its auxiliary G-sharp, and sustained by horns and later by trumpets and other instruments. Sometimes the magical tone sounds from afar, sometimes it is flung out a mighty pæan of praise, with all the instruments' power and glory.

For the finale, Beethoven makes Homeric horseplay with a melody in the character of an Irish folk-tune. The finale takes on the character of a cosmic reel. Jocose ditties stagger through the orchestra and cavort into space—the cat and the fiddle, the cow that jumped over the moon! Toward the end Beethoven resorts again to the device of a persistent bass such as he used so magnificently in the first movement.

"The Grand Symphony in A, one of my very best," said Beethoven.

At the first performance of this symphony, December 18, 1813, at a concert for the benefit of Austrian and Bavarian soldiers disabled at the battle of Hanau, a piece by Beethoven, "Wellington's Victory, or the Battle of Vittoria," arranged for Mälzel's machine, the panharmonican, was also played. Many celebrated musicians were in Vienna, and they were called upon to give their services in the orchestra. Salieri and Hummel played the "cannon" in "Wellington's Victory." The composer Spohr, the violinist Schuppanzigh, and the celebrated Dragonetti, the double-bass player, were among those who took part. Meyerbeer, then a young man, played the bassdrum. He was nervous. Beethoven, who conducted, said afterwards, "Ha! ha! ha! I was not at all satisfied with him; he never struck on the beat; he was always too late, and I was obliged to speak to him rudely. Ha! ha! ha! I could do nothing with him; he did not have the courage to strike on the beat!"

Symphony No. 8, in F major, Opus 93

I. Allegro vivace e con brio
II. Allegretto scherzando
III. Tempo di minuetto
IV. Allegro vivace

Beethoven's Eighth symphony is one of the shortest of the Nine, if not the shortest. For this reason it has been called the "little" symphony. But that is misleading, since "little" tends to confuse size with distinction. As a matter of fact, the Eighth symphony was underestimated when it appeared—"Because it is so much better," growled Beethoven.

Commonly it is believed that such and such a thing happens, that thereupon the composer, "inspired" by the event, sits down in a creative frenzy and pens a masterpiece. Now that has occurred. But more often the reverse is true. Composers produce music which has nothing to do with events. Why? Because music comes from a source deeper in ourselves than we know, and art is an escape from actuality. The conditions under which the Eighth symphony came into existence were in complete contrast to its character. Beethoven, with customary unreasonableness, had quarreled with Mälzel, his good friend who was partly responsible for the symphony; he was profoundly depressed by the mortal illness and financial need of one of his brothers, while he now undertook to interfere with outrageous effrontery in the love affair of another.

This brother was Johann,[1] a successful apothecary, whose smug life the composer despised. Johann had developed an affair, not precisely platonic, with a young woman officially his housekeeper. Beethoven, hearing of this, sped from Teplitz, where he had conversed with Goethe, to Linz, where Johann lived, and promptly there was trouble. Johann received Ludwig hospitably, giving him pleasant rooms overlooking the Danube River. The composer went straight to the point. He demanded that Therese Obermeyer, said housekeeper, comely if not beautiful of person, be put out. Johann suggested, with a fair show of logic, that Ludwig mind his business. There was a violent, an unprintable row. Then Beethoven took the matter to the local authorities and the Bishop. He secured an order that the girl leave town. But the apothecary played to win. He up and married her. The bourgeois romance come to its bourgeois end, Beethoven left in a towering rage for Vienna, having precipitated a disaster in his brother's life, and completed his symphony. He was now so deaf that when he conducted the orchestra he made a ludicrous figure, crouching almost to the ground for the musicians to play softly, leaping into the air for a climax, unable to hear the soft passages, and therefore sometimes losing his place in

[1] It was Johann who, having acquired a handsome property, called on his brother, leaving his card on which was inscribed Johann van Beethoven, Gutsbesitzer (land proprietor), which card Beethoven quickly returned, after writing on the back: Ludwig van Beethoven, Hirnbesitzer (brain proprietor)!

the score. And from all these, and heaven knows what other confusions in his great and stormy soul, came the sunlight and laughter of the Eighth symphony.

Is there rage, frustration, discordant passion in the score? Not one particle. The symphony is sheer joy and release—the laughter of a Titan who elected for the moment to make play with the stars and the planets. In no other work is Beethoven more completely and recklessly the master. The audacity and extravagance of his invention are without end, being subject, at the same time, to a supreme command of form and technic. The first phrase bursts without a preliminary chord or measure or rest from the orchestra, and that's the soul of the man Beethoven, conversing with the wind and sky. I can see him as he often was, in a "raptus," striding through street and field, muttering, shouting, singing, forging his music. The material of the movement does not seem so tremendous until it begins to grow upon you. All sorts of little scraps of sing-song are turned to Beethoven's audacious purposes, which, throughout, are light-hearted, energetic, playful, and audacious in modulation.

The second movement of the symphony has a special connotation. It has to do with Johann Nepomuk Mälzel and the instrument by which he achieved immortality—that instrument which is the curse of the child's music hour, the metronome. In this movement is heard the ticking of the metronome, or rather of its immediate predecessor, Mälzel's musical chronometer.

The metronome ticked; the chronometer, a mechanism in which a "small lever set in motion by a toothed
wheel," caused "little blows on a wooden anvil," must
have tocked. Tick or tock, that monotonously regular
beat was surely in Beethoven's mind when he composed this famous movement, this *jeu d'esprit*, the Allegretto scherzando of the Eighth symphony. The
effect reverses the conventional order of instrumentation, for the wind instruments instead of the strings
carry the accompaniment and tick the measure. There
was a night when Beethoven, Mälzel and other inti-
mates of the composer dined together. According to
Schindler, sometimes inaccurate as a biographer, this
dinner took place before Beethoven went to Linz to
make trouble and compose his symphony. Mälzel was
then planning a trip to England. Beethoven was fond
of writing facetious canons (the canon being a device
of musical imitation, in which a given motive, intoned
by a leading voice, is imitated, in turn, by the other
voice-parts of the composition) and singing them.
On the occasion in question Beethoven jotted down a
canon to the text of farewell, "Ta-Ta-Ta, Lieber
Mälzel," and the company sang the piece with gusto.
This canon, as well as the beat of the musical chronometer, finds its way into the allegretto of the Eighth
symphony. Some historians set the date of the dinner
later than that of the symphony. Be this as it may,
dinner before symphony, symphony before dinner,
the movement is not to be dissociated from Mälzel

and his instrument and Beethoven in a vein of sly humor.

Like the Seventh, this symphony is too light-footed and mercurial to have any slow movement. The third movement is a minuet; but notice how Beethoven's virile spirit transforms the character of the polite dance-form of Haydn or Mozart. The first part of the minuet of the Eighth symphony has the sharp accent, the rude vigor and swing which only Beethoven could give it; but the song given the two horns and clarinets in the quieter contrasting section is divine. At the beginning of the minuet is heard a horn-call, Beethoven's recollection, it is said, of the posthorn of the coach which drove him from Teplitz. Perhaps the last movement of the symphony was the most startling of all to Beethoven's colleagues. To-day it seems that the veriest pedant could not resist applauding his antics. He roars with laughter, he shouts to the heavens, and every measure is an astonishment. Nowhere is he more unbuttoned, more abandoned, yet simple and transparent in style. But even Berlioz, a brilliant critic, a composer far ahead of his time, was puzzled by it. No one wrote more penetratingly of Beethoven as a rule than he. Yet he is slightly apologetic about the Eighth symphony, especially its finale. "All this," he says, "is very curious." He stood too near the Titan who laughed. Sir George Grove, who came later than Berlioz, reserves his highest praise of the symphony for this movement. "The Finale, however, is the great movement of the Symphony. It is pure Beethoven in his most individual and characteristic vein, full of those surprises and sudden unexpected effects, those mixtures of tragedy and comedy, not to say farce, which makes his music so true a mirror of human life, equal in his branch of art to the great plays of Shakespeare in his,—and for the same reasons." It is possible that some of the rhythmic combinations in this finale—groups of two notes against three, et cetera were taken to heart by Brahms, who loved this device. But even Brahms could not hope to write an Eighth symphony.

•

Symphony No. 9, in D minor, with Final Chorus on Schiller's Ode "To Joy," Op. 125

    I.   Allegro ma non troppo, un poco maestoso
   II.   Molto vivace; Presto
  III.   Adagio molto e cantabile; Andante moderato
  IV.   Allegro assai. Quartet and Chorus

The imposing proportions of the Ninth symphony, with its chorale finale which chants the brotherhood of man, give the work a special place among Beethoven's creations and a special consideration on the part of the public. But the colossal work has other claims to greatness.

None of Beethoven's compositions came readily from his pen; this one represented a long and tortuous gestation. It seems that the composer's plan was not completely clear to himself until three-quarters of the symphony had been created. He was in doubt particularly as to the form which the finale should take. This is not surprising, since the Ninth symphony is partly symphony and partly cantata, and the combining of the two styles was a problem even more perplexing in Beethoven's day than it would be in ours. In fact, Wagner found here the tacit acknowledgment on Beethoven's part that the symphony had gone as far as it could without the addition of song and dramatic idea to the instrumental scheme, and this conclusion influenced Wagner profoundly in his course as a composer of opera.

The Ninth symphony appears as a magnificently imperfect creation; as imperfect, let us say, as some tremendous torso of a Michelangelo which implies more by its very pathos and imperfection than a composition neatly and successfully perfected could do. Certainly this is the most profoundly subjective of Beethoven's symphonic utterances. In the pages of his symphonies he is universal rather than personal. His most introspective musings he reserved for the last piano sonatas and string quartets. But here in the Ninth symphony—at least in its first and third movements—is Beethoven himself peering through chaos in loneliness and need seeking a path. No circumstance could have been more symbolic of the master's situation in life and in art than the occasion of the first performance and the tableau presented to the audience: Beethoven standing on the stage, his head sunk on his breast, beating time for the orchestra (which had been warned to disregard his motions); surrounded by silence; unaware that the music had ceased, when he was turned about by one of the singers, Fräulein Unger, to perceive the multitude shouting and with many persons in tears.

The symphony opens with vagueness and suspense, the famous "empty fifths" vibrating softly from the strings. Fragments of the great stark theme that is to come flash across the darkness, and suddenly the orchestra, in gigantic bare unisons, hurls it forth—the Word! One can think of Genesis: "And the earth was without form and void. And God said, 'Let there be light.'" Immense enfoldments follow. The musical material is now grim and tremendous, now singing and tender. It is developed in great detail, yet without the obscuring of vast lines. The return after Exposition and Development to the Recapitulation is especially tremendous, when, over roaring drums, fragments of the great theme hurtle together and flash and splinter, as lightning might strike in a mountain gorge. The ending is pathetic, with the notes of the heroic theme flung out over sullen basses which roll like an ocean after the storm.

The second movement sets a powerful rhythm a-working. It has a gigantic simplicity and dynamic force. The universe dances. Imitations, foreshortenings, extensions of the dance figure, are in Beethoven's most concentrated style. The trio, a passage of starry serenity, was composed before the rest of the movement. When the earlier part of the scherzo returns, there are further rhythmic transformations. Blows of the kettledrums, solo, fortissimo, interrupt the rhythm with characteristic energy and brusquerie, an effect which caused the audience at the first performance to applaud in the midst of the movement.

In the slow movement Beethoven dispenses with strict form. The movement has two lyrical themes, which are heard in alternation, with variants of one of them. "As to the beauty of these melodies," wrote Hector Berlioz, "the infinite grace of the ornaments applied to them, the sentiments of melancholy, tenderness and passionate sadness and of religious meditation which they express—if my prose could give all this even an approximate idea, music would have found in the written word such a competitor as even the greatest of all poets was never able to oppose to it. It is an immense work; and, when once its powerful charm has been experienced, the only answer for the critic who reproaches the composer for having violated the law of unity is 'So *much the worse for the law.*'"

The conception of a symphony with a chorale finale had long been forming in the master's consciousness. As a youth of twenty-three he had attempted a setting of Schiller's "Ode," but the theme he then created had nothing to do with that of the Ninth symphony. Nor was the theme of the finale the only problem which confronted him. How connect in a natural and logical manner the choral conclusion with the preceding movements? That was the crux of the problem. The Beethoven's sketch-books, extraordinary documents of his creative life, tell us of his struggle. He seems to have decided that some preliminary words must introduce the passages for chorus and quartet. What words were they to be? The sketch-books are littered with fragmentary musical motives and phrases of text.

Thus, over the notation of a musical phrase of recitative: "No, these . . . remind of our despair." And later, "My fri . . . let it be celebrated with . . ." and more musical notation. Farther on, "Oh not this . . . something . . . but only a little merrier . . . (nor this either it is but sport, or no better) . . . (nor this it is too tender) . . . (for something animated we must seek) . . . (I shall see to it that I myself intone something then do you sing after me) . . . This it is ha now it is found I myself will intone it. . . . Ha this is it now is discovered . . . Freu . . . meilleur." And later the memorandum, words and notes, with which Beethoven rushed into a room one day crying out to Schindler (according to that gentleman's recollection), "I have it! I have it! Let us sing the song of the immortal Schiller Freude!" He had been, in these days, more than ever preoccupied, suspicious, a lone wolf among his kind. But he had found what he was seeking. The remaining months of 1823 saw the completion of the symphony, which was first performed in Vienna, March 7, 1824.

The finale, close upon the mystery and exaltation of the preceding movement, opens with a terrific hullabaloo of the instruments, highly discordant, which is answered by an admonishing recitative of cellos and basses. But these instruments are helpless in their attempt at pacification. The racket bursts out again. A shorter conciliating phrase of the recitative proposes, as a solution, some measures of the introduction. These too are furiously dismissed. Then, in answer to persistent summons, a fragment of the scherzo is heard. It is rejected, but more gently, and now there is anticipation of the theme of the "Ode to Joy." After one more gesture of recitative, it is given extended statement by the orchestra.

Observe how Beethoven, whose ideas came to him in symphonic and not in vocal guise, clings to his instruments. No sooner, however, has the choral subject received its symphonic endorsement than the orchestra is seized with fresh rebellion. It howls more loudly and terribly than ever; two opposed chords, shrieking to high heaven, sound at once all the notes of the harmonic minor scale!

This clears the air. Now the solo baritone propounds a sentiment to the melody of the recitative earlier sounded by instruments:

"O brothers, let us have no more of these sad tones. Let us rejoice together." The basses of the chorus, the solo quartet, the full chorus, expand the theme. Thereafter come sundry variations and interludes for solo voices, for quartet, for chorus. The solo tenor, with the chorus, sings a march movement, inspired by the thoughts of "heroes" and "victory" in Schiller's text. A passage for full chorus apostrophizes the united, advancing millions, and the stars that form the canopy of the Father's dwelling in the heavens. The mood becomes more jubilant, with brilliant passages for the vocal ensemble against rushing instrumental figures. The pace quickens. There are shouts, "Hail thee, Joy, from heaven descending," and so ends the Ninth symphony and Beethoven's dream of an advancing liberated mankind.

CARL MARIA von WEBER

1786–1826

Overture to "Der Freischütz"

THE overture to "Der Freischütz" is the prelude to a romantic opera. It is so romantic and youthful that when it sounds, the youngest of us can feel cold-blooded and calculating, and bend the knee to an art poetical and aglow with a deathless flame. In the last thirty years there have been some thrilling first performances, but I would exchange most of the premières I have attended for that one—to have sat in with the young generation, and the poets and patriots who stirred to the new music, hearing in it, with sudden, incredulous joy, the things they had despaired of ever hearing, though they had held them sacred and inviolate in themselves. For the overture to "Der Freischütz," to the German audiences of 1821,[1] was a song of deliverance from a black-shadowed past, and the emblem of a new day.

[1] There were performances of the overture before the opera saw the stage. The first of these took place at Copenhagen, Oct. 8, 1820, when Weber was touring North Germany and Denmark. The first performance of the opera was at Berlin, June 18, 1821.

There is no need here to go into historical detail, save to remark that the composition of "Der Freischütz" was synchronous in Germany with the throwing off a foreign yoke and a resulting new national consciousness in art. And I remember the saying of someone, whose name I have forgotten, that he did not care who made a nation's laws if he could make its songs. Armies had won Germany her freedom, statesmen were plotting and planning the empire that was to crumble in the evil days of "balance of power." Armies, statesmen and Empire have vanished. What remains of that day of youth and dawn is immortally sung by Weber and artists of his age.

The other day I came across Wagner's reference in his autobiography to the indelible impression this music made upon him when, as a boy, he refused to study but would sit at the piano and bang away at the "Freischütz" overture; when his stepfather, slowly dying, heard the problematic Richard thumping a ditty in the next room, and turned to his wife, saying, "Is it possible that he has musical talent?" when, later on, the ghosts of Weber and Beethoven appeared in a dream to the composer-to-be and urged him on. And Wagner speaks of the sensation of mystery and suspense he experienced when he heard the opening C of this overture, intoned softly by the strings. That C was to inspire other composers than Wagner. It struck from German operatic art the shackles of a foreign culture. It liberated her lyric theater from

[89]

the domination of the Italian style—a thing which even such giants as Mozart and Beethoven had been unable to do. It admitted nature, which hitherto had been kept at a respectful distance, to the opera house. And it created a whole school of music drama in Weber's train.

The opera is based on a folk-tale of the Black Forest. It tells of the deliverance of the young hunter, *Max,* from the snares of Satan and the bullets which destroy not only men's bodies but souls. He is saved by the love and faith of *Agatha,* his betrothed. The jubilant conclusion of the overture connotes the victory of young love, the confusion of the Fiend, and rejoicing of the people.

The overture begins with that C which so impressed Wagner's imagination, and a short phrase which branches from it, singularly evocative of the fragrance of the forest. The horn quartet plays a solemn chorale, symbol of faith and prayer. And now a shadow falls over the orchestra, with the tremolo of the strings, pluckings of the basses, and a prophesying 'cello—premonition of evil. This is the introduction. The main body of the overture opens with agitation and storm. A passage which excited the admiration of Hector Berlioz, the French composer, is as thrilling today as it was to him in the Twenties. It comes with the wild outcry of the horns, three times repeated, and the clarinet that wails over the vibrating strings. In the opera this phrase is sung by *Max* as, at midnight, he stares down in terror at the devilish incantations in the Wolf's Glen. In the overture the effect, without the words, without the scene, is even more appealing to the imagination. "O Weber!" cries Berlioz, in his "Treatise on Instrumentation," apostrophizing this evocation of "distance, echo . . . twilight sound." He says elsewhere that this theme moves him "incomparably more than all the rest. It strikes home to the heart, and for me at least, this virginal song, which seems to breathe skyward a timid reproach, while a somber harmony shudders and threatens, is one of the most novel, poetic and beautiful contrasts that modern art has produced in music." Soon after, as if in response to the clarinet, an exultant air is played softly by the strings. Then more tumult. Then, for the last time, the shadow again creeping over the orchestra. But this is not to be. There is a pause, and a shout of triumph—emergence forever from the darkness into the day, into the sun—and the apotheosis, with the chivalric flourishes, so characteristic of Weber, of the triumphal song.

This "Freischütz" overture, which flung open the doors to so much that was new in music, is prophetic of the whole art of modern instrumentation. In Weber's orchestra, as never before, each instrument has its individuality, is inhabited by a special demon who does the master's bidding. The tone-tints are combined with as much variety as a painter's colors are combined on his palette. Even Beethoven, a greater

composer than Weber, and one who wrought great
changes in the orchestra, had not Weber's modern
sense of tone-color and instinct for the picturesque.
Here in the "Freischütz" overture is nature-painting,
vivid, instantaneous—not a conventionalized canvas,
not a design in black and white, but a tone-picture of
the forest itself, the tossing trees, the song of the
wind, the mystery of the night. True, the demons in-
habiting this orchestra are tamer today than they
were in Weber's time. We are not terrified by them.
His music is actually very simple and for that reason
the more appropriate to the naïve folk-tale. But it is
epochal. We cannot overestimate the genius of it, or
sufficiently venerate its purity and freshness of inspiration. Here, indeed, is the fountain that Ponce de
Leon sought. O Weber! your genius, your youth,
your vision of the dawn!

FRANZ PETER SCHUBERT

1797–1828

Symphony in B minor ("Unfinished")

I. Allegro moderato
II. Andante con moto

SCHUBERT composed his "Unfinished" symphony when he was twenty-five, when the tragedy of his short, humble and poverty-stricken life was eating into his soul. There is the story that he composed the two movements in gratitude for having been elected an honorary member of a music society of Linz. Only a little time before he had been hurt and bitterly discomfited by the refusal of the Society of the Friends of Music of Vienna, based on a technicality, to admit him to membership. We know this latter thing to be true, and we know of poor Schubert's gratification when the smaller and less important society accepted him. As for the question of his purpose in composing the fragments of the "Unfinished," the facts, as modern research has proved, disagree with the legend; but the principle involved in the legend holds true as a revelation of Schubert's character. He could have done just that. He could also have written these incomparable movements for no purpose whatever save relieving his mind of the pressure of inspiration. He could have tucked them in a drawer and forgotten them because of the importunities of new ideas always thronging through the mind of a man whose creative fertility has become proverbial, who thought nothing of composing eight songs in a day, and whose creative fever burnt him up in his thirty-first year. Also—what remains perfectly possible—there might be in existence, in some hiding-place, the two missing movements of the "Unfinished" symphony. They might still turn up, as new Schubert manuscripts often turn up, for his productivity was incredible.

The story of the discovery of the "Unfinished" symphony, which Schubert never heard, is a curious one. It is told by the conductor Anton Herbeck, the man who took the music from its hiding-place and made it known to the world. Herbeck had been apprised by Josef Hüttenbrenner, an intimate friend of Schubert's youth, years after Schubert's death, that Josef's brother, Anselm, who fancied himself considerably as a creative musician, possessed many Schubert manuscripts—among them, said Josef, a "B minor symphony, which we put on a level with the great symphony in C, his instrumental swan song, and any one of the great symphonies of Beethoven." For some years Herbeck had put this matter aside, but in 1865, thirty-seven years after Schubert had died, Herbeck was in Graz, Styria, on a trip for his health, and he decided, if possible, to secure the symphony. He encountered Anselm, old and infirm, at an inn

[94]

where the quondam friend of Schubert was in the habit of breakfasting. The two men spoke together, then repaired to the tumble-down cottage where the toothless Anselm was passing his last days. Herbeck said that he wanted to give a concert consisting of the works of three contemporaries, "Schubert, Hütten-brenner and Lachner. It would be excellent if Schubert could be represented by a new work." Anselm gave Herbeck the choice of any one of ten overtures which he had composed, and added: "I have still a lot of things by Schubert. Look them over and help yourself." Herbeck, if he felt excitement, concealed it as his eyes fell on the MS. of the B minor symphony. He said, "This would do. Will you let me have it copied?" and Anselm replied, "There's no hurry. Take it with you." And so it was that Schubert's "Unfinished" symphony made its first public appearance on a program between an overture by one Hüttenbrenner and a set of songs, not by Lachner, but by Herbeck, who was apparently willing to figure in such company!

In addition to the two movements which Herbeck had unearthed, there were 130 measures of a third movement, of which nine were orchestrated. The photographic reproductions of Schubert's manuscript display the two movements and the fragment of the third in replica.

Nevertheless, it is difficult to believe that the third part belongs to the others. An examination of the reputed third movement of the B minor symphony upholds the view of Herbert F. Peyser, who, in an article upon the history of the B minor symphony, in the "Musical Quarterly" of October, 1928, concludes that the few measures of the third movement do not belong to the completed movements at all; that they are decidedly inferior to the first and second and that the *prima facie* evidence points to an entirely different origin of the extra measures. Could they not have been found in the same pile of music paper and by mistake included with the other two movements of the symphony? Whatever the explanation, the two movements that exist are among the highest creative flights Schubert ever took, and are the most concise and concentrated in their workmanship of all his symphonic writings. They show what might have happened if Schubert could have lived the allotted span of mortal years and received a tithe of the attention and encouragement given to his contemporary Beethoven.

It was given to Schubert to answer human experience with music of a beauty that gives us ineffable consolation and surcease from pain. The somber and purely Schubertian phrase for the 'cellos and basses which makes the introduction is a confounding stroke of genius, establishing, in ten measures, mood and a thematic corner-stone of the movement. Then we hear the murmuring accompaniment of the strings that reminded Schubert's admirable biographer, Ed-

monstoune Duncan, of the sea. Over the tossing figure
the oboe sings its haunting complaint. The same astonishing conciseness noted in the introduction is observed by the preparation for the second theme with
a few chords of the strings and the sustained tone of
the horn. Everything in the symphony is the essence
of Schubert, and the second theme for the 'cellos is
one of his sheer inspirations. Passages of its development are wildly dramatic and at the end the phrase of
the introduction returns with a stripped tragic power
worthy of Beethoven.

How divinely far from the world of men is Schubert's slow movement with its strange peace, its rapt
meditation and compassion, its prescience of another
sphere!

It would be a pleasure, and useful as a background
for this symphony, to say much of Schubert himself,
his simplicity, his loving-kindness, his essential solitude, in the midst of unceremonious friends and boon
companions that he loved; his pathetic need; his bitter griefs, of which he complained only in terms of
song; the singular purity of his soul. Also his pranks
and impromptu performances as pianist, when he
would improvise waltzes and country-dances for
good company at an inn in the mountains; his
good-natured fury because he could not play the difficult finale of his own "Wanderer" fantasy; the dis-
mal lodgings with the poet Mayrhofer; the days when
Schubert wore his spectacles to bed in order that he

might be ready to go on with his composing the instant he awakened; the clothes he shared in common with companions as poverty-stricken as himself; his happy escapes from the society of aristocrats to that of peasants and housemaids; his performances of his song "The Erl-king" on a hair-comb. There never was so lovable and improvident a man, unless it was Mozart, and even Mozart knew more of the world and the ways of great society. Schubert, after the funeral of Beethoven, whom he adored, drank a toast to the one of his group who should be the next to go. That one was Schubert himself, and a few days before his death a friend rushed out and sold a number of his greatest songs for a few cents apiece. Schubert once said, "My music is the product of my genius and my misery, and that which I have written in my greatest distress is that which seems best to the world." But the epitaph, more poignant than any other could possibly be, of this life cut short, is the "Unfinished" symphony.

●

Symphony No. 7 in C major

I.   Andante; Allegro ma non troppo
II. Andante con moto
III. Scherzo: Allegro vivace; Trio
IV. Finale: Allegro vivace

The "Unfinished" and C major symphonies are the ones of the ten that Schubert composed which survive him. The other symphonies, in greater or lesser degree, are formative. These two are without a parallel in symphonic literature. In a way they supplement each other. The one is a song of which humanity can know the beginning, but never the end; the other is one of the most sublime outpourings of joy in the literature of music.

The great Schubert C major symphony lasts for nearly an hour of wonderful sound. The composer's inspiration does not flag for a moment. The solo horn that opens the work sings its way straight into the blue. This melody, characterized at first by an Olympic serenity, winds through different registers and choirs of the orchestra. As the mood becomes more exultant, counter-figures are wreathed about it. It is flung out mightily by instruments in unison. Calls from afar echo thunderously down corridors of space and time.

The tempo quickens, to usher in the main body of the movement, which, above all, and like the rest of the symphony, is a play of rhythms. For this is the symphony which, more than any other, merits the title Wagner gave Beethoven's Seventh—"The Apotheosis of the Dance."

The opening theme combines within itself two rhythms, a decisive beat in "two" time, and a triplet figure that leaves the earth with a rapturous flutter of wings. The two rhythms sound sometimes in succession and sometimes simultaneously, until preparation is made for the second theme. This is a dance measure, the melody given wind instruments, with whirling accompaniment figures for the strings—an orchestral device often found in this symphony. And thereafter songs pour from the instruments in such profusion that there is scarcely time for the development of one idea before another crowds swiftly upon it. The movement ends with the orchestra intoning in great unison the theme of the introduction.

In the slow movement there is the tinge of Hungarian melancholy which affected every great composer who lived in Vienna, saving only the deaf Beethoven, who could not hear the gypsies. The oboe, after some introductory passages by plucked strings, intones a melody in the minor key which oboes and clarinets repeat in thirds. The strings respond with a more flowing phrase. Full chords of the orchestra, in march rhythm, are echoed by the woodwinds. A new and dreaming phrase for the strings is heard, followed by the horn, of which Schumann spoke when he said, probably referring to this place, that it "seems to come from another sphere, while everything listens, as though some heavenly messenger were hovering around the orchestra." When the march is resumed the motion is augmented by extra rhythmical figures played by trumpets, horns and other accompanying instruments. And now comes the one place in the symphony where tragedy lifts its head and utters a sharp cry of pain. It is a passage of shattering drama, a cry of agony, suddenly broken off, and followed by a pause of silence. Then the solo cello is heard, an answer of infinite tenderness. The music modulates into the major tonality. In due course the minor key returns and the march theme files off in the distance.

The scherzo, grandly designed like all the rest of the symphony, begins with a vigorous peasant step, and exuberant gayety. The contrasting middle part, the trio, is a melody which epitomizes all that is poetical, sentimental, nostalgic, in the nature of the Viennese, of whom Schubert was one. The starry evening! The swaying dance! Or, let us say, the purpling hills and the wistful thoughts of the little man who, so far as we know, never experienced woman's love, though he dreamed and sang of it in unforgettable strains.

What could be done after all this? What only Schubert could do! His finale is Dionysiac. The orchestra is possessed of an intoxication only matched by the potency of the ideas. It is a vertiginous whirl of inspiration—the dance-apotheosis. Toward the end four great C's, an intensive rhythmical development of the accompaniment figure of the second theme, earlier announced, are sounded in earth-shaking unison by massed instruments, as if winged Pegasus, poised for his flight, stamped the world in his impatience and joy. Shouts of the entire orchestra answer him; the symphony sweeps tumultuously to its close. It is all prodigious past the telling.

No more than the "Unfinished" was Schubert to hear this last of his symphonies. He is said to have intended it for the Musikverein of Vienna, which found the composition too difficult to play. It was performed by the Gesellschaft der Musikfreunde, December 14, 1828, a few weeks after Schubert's death. It was repeated by the same body a year later, and then lay forgotten until Schumann visited Schubert's brother Ferdinand in 1838 and sent a copy of the symphony to Mendelssohn in Leipsic. He, making some cuts in it, gave it repeated and successful interpretations.

This music is so simple and so frank that at first you may take it for granted. The better you know it, the more impressive it becomes. Though it follows generally classical precedent, it is not a work of the Beethoven tradition. That was left for Brahms to carry on. Because of its completeness as well as its prodigious inspiration this symphony of Schubert's is perhaps the only work of sufficient greatness before Brahms to take a commanding position in the wake of the immortal Nine.

HECTOR BERLIOZ

1803–1869

"Fantastic" Symphony, Opus 14-A

I.   Dreams, Passions (Largo; Allegro agitato e appassionato assai)
II. A Ball (Valse: Allegro non troppo)
III. Scene in the Fields (Adagio)
IV. March to the Scaffold (Allegretto non troppo)
V.   Witches' Sabbath (Larghetto; Allegro)

B UT now there steps proudly and defiantly across the stage of history a red-haired madman who was one of the most audacious composers that ever lived— Hector Berlioz, the composer of the "Fantastic" symphony. There is something very splendid about him, and very heroic, and a little ridiculous and pathetically lonely. He had little musical background, and was not more than half-trained in his art when, as a calf of twenty-six, he fell desperately in love with an Irish actress, and observed the momentous event by producing a convulsive symphony which affected a whole century of music. Berlioz had nobody to help him in this task, no kindly and discerning critic, no model to go by, for the simple reason that nobody had dreamed of such a score. But he was fortunately quite mad in his attitude toward art and the expression of life, and, where his personal affairs and ideas were

[103]

concerned, magnificently without humor. Otherwise he never could have projected his symphony.

The "Symphonie Fantastique" came of an era of quixotry and exhibitionism, but also greatness; and I could wish that life had for us the gorgeous hues that it wore for Berlioz and his fellow-romantics. They were the young men of 1830 in Paris, then a hotbed of strange artistic blooms. They were born, wrote Alfred de Musset in his "Confession of a Child of the Century," of unquiet mothers who had never been far from the rolling drums and the roaring cannon of the Napoleonic wars. The ashes of the French Revolution were still smoldering. The ideas of Rousseau which had so much to do with that upheaval were rampant, and were mixed with all sorts of exotic trends of thought. The oceans were now completely traversed. The imaginations of men roamed to far distant lands. The young generation was overwrought by the nervous and emotional strains through which the race had passed; at the same time it was inflamed and exalted by new democratic, socialistic, humanitarian currents of the day. As citizens had thrown off the bonds of despotic government, so were the poets, dramatists, musicians of the new order determined to think and create, each man for himself, according to his own dreams and desires. Hence the more extravagant, the more wildly individualistic the conception, the better. They wore long hair, these young men, fierce mustachios, and red waistcoats, like the one that Théophile Gautier wore at the première of Victor Hugo's "Hernani." The millennium was at hand; they were to forge by means of their art the ideas of a new state of society. The marvelous thing is what they actually accomplished, with all their struttings and rhetoric. Since the period of the Renaissance the world had not looked at life so richly, so impetuously. And Paris? It was not a hotbed, it was a conflagration of genius. In those days there walked the streets Hugo and Balzac and Heine and Delacroix, de Musset, Gautier, Dumas, Liszt, Meyerbeer, Rossini, Paganini, Chopin, George Sand—if I should turn to a chronicle of those days and name all the artistic figures of the epoch from 1830 to 1840, those native to the city and the country, and all the others who came from afar to the Mecca of art, such as Wagner, the list would be five times extended. Such was the background and breeding-place of Berlioz's "Fantastic" symphony.

Berlioz, the son of a doctor, incorrigibly an artist, who read Virgil, Lamartine, Chateaubriand and James Fenimore Cooper, and knew the names of the islands of the South Seas better than he did those of the Departments of France, came to Paris at the age of twenty-one and undertook courses in medicine. But not for long. He quickly jumped through the window of the dissecting room, and took to music as a fish which disappears in its native element. After the laboratory he lived the life of an impecunious dreamer and firebrand in Paris; plunged into the scores of Gluck, Weber, Beethoven and a few other composers, whom he intimately comprehended and adored; learned instrumentation, of which he became one of the greatest masters, at first hand from scores and from players in orchestras; took valuable lessons in composition from a truly sympathetic soul at the Paris Conservatoire—Lesueur—and was chased around the table of the Conservatoire library by stanch old Cherubini, who hated him. Then he saw the Irish actress, Henrietta Smithson, act Shakespeare, and was gone, lost, demented with love. According to the story he said: "That woman shall be my wife, and on that drama I shall write my greatest symphony." The story is in no whit incredible. Young men have talked that way before. The incredible thing, like other deeds of the romantics, is the symphony.

Berlioz wooed Miss Smithson wildly. He made her life a burden. He tried to poison himself in her presence and nearly succeeded. He had first beheld her as *Ophelia* in 1827. He began to dream of the great symphony which he would compose for her, advancing in the world by her side. At first she was indifferent to him. She said she liked him "well enough," which maddened our Hector of the flaming locks, as James Huneker called him. Miss Smithson went to London in 1829, and slanderous stories about her drove Berlioz insane, so that, according to legend, he wandered for two days, without food, without sleep, in desolate fields outside of Paris. He completed his symphony in 1830. It was an open letter, a reproach and an insult to Miss Smithson. In the last movement of the work he portrayed her as a vile courtesan in Hades, and, lest there should be any mistake about it, he furnished the score with a literary program which was explicit. Berlioz tried to secure the actress' presence at the performance. "I hope the wretched woman will be there," wrote our anguished romantic. "I do not believe it, however; she will surely recognize herself in reading the program of my instrumental drama, and she will take care not to appear." There was a mammoth orchestra. There were 2300 pages of music to be copied for the players, and the cost to Berlioz was far more than his purse could stand. Miss Smithson did not hear the symphony. That came later.

In 1832, after disastrous appearances in London, poor, at her wit's end, anxious if possible to open her own theater in Paris, the actress returned to the French capital. She received an invitation to go to a concert. With nothing else to do, she took a carriage, read the "program" of the symphony, which Berlioz had fortunately modified, remembered his desperate avowals and his incredible acts, and was flattered. This was one of the great moments of the romantic Paris. Heine, Dumas, Hugo were in the audience. So was Adolphe Nourrit, the celebrated tenor who was to create leading rôles in Meyerbeer's "Huguenots" and "Robert le Diable." So was Paganini. Miss Smithson sat in her box, and Berlioz, seated before the kettledrums, frowned in the orchestra. Also present was Fétis, the critic, sworn foe of Berlioz and his tribe. The program consisted of the "Symphonie Fantastique," which is but the first part of a work entitled "Episode in the Life of an Artist," and its sequel, a melodrama, "Lelio; or, the Return to Life." This last work required the services of an orator, and he was the actor Bocage. Bocage made an address. In doing so he deliberately imitated the speech and the gestures of Fétis in such a way that there was laughter, and all eyes were turned toward the critic of the "Temps" and the "Revue Musicale." The speech was punctuated with the audience's applause as Bocage grew heated in his eloquence, spouting furiously such gems of rhetoric as the following: "May they [the old school] be accursed! They outrage art in the most ridiculous fashion! Like those common birds which inhabit our public gardens . . . when they have put filth on the forehead of Jupiter or the breast of Venus, they exhibit themselves proud and satisfied, as if they had just laid a golden egg!" And more of the same. The performance proceeded. Heine observed that every time Berlioz caught Miss Smithson's eye he gave a furious roll on the drums—which chronicle must be a little romantic in itself, if one pauses to reflect that kettledrums play notes of certain pitch, and are used at certain times in a given score, and that if

Berlioz had rolled them at any chance moment he would have greatly distorted the effect of his symphony. This we may be sure he did not do. Heine wrote later, after Berlioz's marriage to Miss Smithson, that he had cut his hair, and no longer rolled furiously upon the kettledrums. In more ways than one the marriage was disastrous.

But the symphony was a success. It was received with tremendous enthusiasm by those who cried *à bas* with the shackles of ossified tradition and wanted to make art, in their own words, "as much like life as possible."

"As much like life as possible"! Heaven save the mark! Listen to the plot of the "Fantastic" symphony.

First Berlioz informs us—I employ his own words, as translated by William Foster Apthorp—that "A young musician, of morbid sensibility and ardent imagination, poisons himself with opium in a fit of amorous despair. The narcotic dose, too weak to result in death, plunges him into a heavy sleep accompanied by the strangest visions, during which his sensations, sentiments and recollections are translated in his sick brain into musical thoughts and images. The beloved woman herself has become for him a melody, liked a fixed idea which he finds and hears everywhere."

And so we have, at the very beginning of the symphony, the melody which, to composer and listener, is to typify the person of the beloved and the composer's thoughts of her. In the most diverse moods, amid the most diverse scenes, in the five movements of the symphony, this melody, in various transformations, reappears. The first movement is called by Berlioz "Dreams, Passions." It is music of causeless melancholy, anguish, fury, tenderness and "religious consolations." The second is "A Ball." In the midst of the dance the hero seeks his beloved. He sees her and her melody reappears in the orchestra. She is, for programmatic purposes, surrounded by her admirers at a brilliant fête. The third movement is "Scene in the Fields." Wandering in the fields on a summer evening, the musician hears two shepherds playing their pipes. "This pastoral duet, the scene around him, the light rustling of the trees gently swayed by the breeze, some hopes he has recently conceived, all combine to restore an unwonted calm to his heart and to impart a more cheerful coloring to his thoughts; but she appears once more, his heart stops beating, he is agitated with painful presentiments; if she were to betray him! . . . One of the shepherds resumes his artless melody, the other no longer answers him. The sun sets. . . . The sound of distant thunder. . . . Solitude. . . . Silence. . . ."

The fourth movement is the celebrated "March to the Scaffold." The morbid young man, dreaming under the influence of the opium, imagines that he has killed his beloved, that he is condemned to death, and led to execution. "The procession advances to the tones of a march which is now somber and wild, now brilliant and solemn, in which the dull sound of the tread of heavy feet follows without transition upon the most resounding outbursts. At the end the fixed idea appears for a moment, like a last thought of love, interrupted by the fatal stroke."

After supping so full of horrors, what is left for the finale? This: Witches' Sabbath; orgy of witches; monsters, ghosts, celebrating the young man's death. "In the midst of a frightful group who have come together to celebrate his obsequies, he hears strange noises, groans, ringing laughter, shrieks to which other shrieks seem to reply. The beloved melody again appears, but it has lost its noble and timid character, it has become an ignoble, trivial, grotesque dance tune; it is she who comes to the witches' Sabbath . . . howlings of joy at her arrival . . . she takes part in the diabolical orgy. Funeral knells, burlesque parody on the 'Dies iræ.' Witches' dance. The witches' dance and the 'Dies iræ' together."

The "Beloved melody," the obsessing idea, or its musical prototype, is announced at once at the beginning of the symphony, tenderly and dreamily, by the strings. In the second movement, "The Ball," it appears in an interlude between brilliant passages of dance music, and is there introduced by the flute. Various wind instruments have fragments of it in the "Scene in the Field," which is poetical, but long drawn out for our day. The movement closes with fragments of the shepherd's song and the rolling of distant thunder. The "March to the Scaffold" is nightmarish. When performed it should be, not in the melodramatic manner but in half-veiled sonorities, through which, suddenly and deafeningly, cut savage howls and blares of the brass, the music has the character of the disordered vision of the opium-eater. Notice, about two-thirds through the march, the evil chucklings of the bassoons, like birds of ill-omen following the procession. With the opening of the "Witches' Sabbath" the theme of the Beloved is heard in a sardonic, distorted dance rhythm. The bells toll for the macabre festivity. The trombones and then the horns, as if in chorus, caricature the terrible old plain-chant, the *"Dies iræ."*

The origin of the Beloved's melody—the musical *idée fixe*—is typical of the romanticist's progress. It was a song which Berlioz composed when he was fifteen years old to an exquisite girl, Estelle Gautier, who was tall, with dark eyes, jet hair, and pretty pink slippers. To Estelle Berlioz composed the melody which, in a later day, came in so handily as the theme song of the work that he created to gain the love of another woman! The melody was properly valued by the composer as the expression of a young heart tortured by longing and passion, as Berlioz, in his memoirs, frankly avers. In later years Berlioz and Estelle were to meet again. Very touching is the letter in which the composer, alone, fatigued with life and the terrible battles he had fought for art, addressed to this same Estelle, become a nice and sensible old lady. The old fellow, after two marital disasters—and how many tragedies?—fell again at the feet of the girl he had once loved and asked her to wed him. She gently, kindly and sensibly refused. You don't read their letters without a moistening of the eyes.

Berlioz's use of the "fixed idea" in his symphony is important and prophetic. We have observed the transplanting of certain thematic material in the hands of Haydn and Beethoven. Berlioz's procedure is dictated by poetical as well as musical consideration. It leads directly to Liszt's practice in his symphonic poems. It precedes Wagner's use of musical "leading motives" to depict characters and ideas in his operas. This is the real beginning of modern program music.

Another epochal characteristic of the "Fantastic" symphony is its orchestration. Where did Berlioz learn this? He had studied profoundly scores of Beethoven, Weber and Gluck, who knew something of tone-painting. The "Pastoral" symphony considerably antedated the "Fantastic." The instrumental schemes of Weber, perhaps nearest those of Berlioz, had struck the authentic note of modern instrumentation. But Berlioz enriched the orchestral palette to an extent that neither Weber nor any other of his predecessors had dreamed.

Fortunately, he could not play proficiently on an

instrument. This was good for him. It freed his musical imagination. It freed him from thinking in any
instrumental or technical patterns. Being the slave of
no one instrument, he was master, by intuition and
the sovereign power of his imagination, of them all.
Neither Strauss, nor Mahler, nor Debussy, nor the
whole Russian school of the late nineteenth century,
could exist, orchestrally speaking, without Berlioz.
All this is predicated by the "Fantastic" symphony.

ROBERT ALEXANDER SCHUMANN

1810–1856

Symphony No. 1, in B flat major, Opus 38

I.   Andante un poco maestoso; Allegro molto vivace
II. Larghetto
III. Scherzo: Molto vivace; Trio I: Molto piu vivace; Trio II
IV. Allegro animato e grazioso

THE most romantic and personal of symphonies are the four by Robert Schumann. They are the outpourings of a young poet's heart, who molds the classic form to his heart's desire.

The ten years of Schumann's career as symphonist were from 1841 to 1851; 1840 was the year of his marriage to Clara Wieck, a happiness which colored all his art. He had waited long for his bride, and had known bitter hours of discouragement and frustration. For once in history a happily consummated romance did inspire a composer. Up to the time of his marriage Schumann had written entirely for the piano. He now literally burst into song, producing by the score a unique series of lieder, and then turned to the symphony. One day he read a poem by Adolph Boettger—a minor German poet, a poem of gloomy cast. Observe how we make our world in accordance with our image of it! The poem begins with a melan-

[115]

choly apostrophe to the "dark storm cloud" and an entreaty that it change its course. It concludes with the line that set Schumann's soul vibrating: "In the valley blooms the Spring."

The best index to the nature of this work is provided in a letter Schumann wrote Wilhelm Tauber who was to conduct a performance of it in Berlin. "Could you infuse," says our tone-poet, "into your orchestra . . . a sort of longing for Spring? . . . The first entrance of the trumpets, this I should like to have sounded as though it were from above, like unto a call to awakening; and then I should like reading between the lines, in the rest of the introduction, how everywhere it begins to grow green, how a butterfly takes wing and, in the allegro, how little by little all things come that in any way belong to Spring. True, these are fantastic thoughts, which only came to me after the work was finished; only, I tell you this about the Finale, that I thought of it as the good-by of Spring."

A trumpet call, as from on high, is answered by a shout from the full orchestra. There is then a growing agitation among the instruments. The joyous tumult leads into the exultant main movement. This opens with a lively version of the initial trumpet motive, of which the rhythm dominates the movement. A march-like rhythm leads to the second theme, a lovely, plaintive phrase given to the clarinets. In the development of the material some subsidiary matter is added, but everything moves to the propulsive energy of the first theme, and it is impossible not to think of mounting sap and universal stir of life.

The return from free development to the first theme is preceded by the proclamation of the introductory trumpet call and the orchestral response. At the end of the recapitulation comes a long-breathed concluding subject, a hymn of thanksgiving for the new life that has come to the earth with the Spring; and again the victorious fanfare sounds from the skies.

Lovers of Schumann have special treasures, and surely a particular place must be given to the dreamily passionate song that makes the burden of the first movement. The melody of the slow movement, possessed of the fervor and languor of Spring, floats like a water-lily on the surface of the orchestral accompaniment; later it is played by the violoncellos with ornamentations of the violins. The movement ends with soft chorale-like harmonies for the trombones, and a gently interrogatory phrase of the clarinet, which is not a conclusion.

For the answer comes, after a short pause, with the virile attack of the scherzo. Scherzo movements in all the Schumann symphonies have a special character, not fantastic or demoniac, like Beethoven's, but rather poetical transfigurations of German folk-dances. Some of the dance rhythms are heavy-footed and redolent of the good soil. Others, less physical, evoke thoughts tender, mocking, gay. Schumann extends these movements beyond the customary proportions of the three-part scherzo form, which has earlier been described. And so in the scherzo of this "Spring" symphony there are two "Trios," or middle parts, with piquant alternations of rhythms and of tempi. Just at the end is a little, unique coda, a teasing afterthought, of the greatest charm.

Schumann has told us his conception of the last movement—the thought of Spring's farewell as she trips onward over the country-side. This is the lightest and perhaps the least of the four movements, but it is delicious. The introductory theme has the inflection of a light-hearted serenade. Now the music hurries, now it dallies. Shouts of horns and wind instruments, over rushing strings, signalize the gay flight.

•

 Symphony in D minor, Opus 120, numbered 4

I.   Andante; Allegro
II. Romanza
III. Scherzo
IV. Largo; Finale

This symphony is actually Schumann's second, revised ten years after its completion in 1841, and then published as the Fourth. It is discussed in this place, not for the sake of chronological exactness, but because its ideas influenced the works that followed. It was conceived in the same year as the "Spring" symphony, and was presented by Robert to Clara on her birthday, September 13, a year and a day after their marriage, and on the baptismal day of their first child. But it is very different from its companion-piece, the "Spring" symphony, being more introspective and more individual in the treatment of the form. No doubt the fact that Schumann revised the work a decade after its conception is partly responsible for this. He then altered both structure and instrumentation. But we know that the revised score is in essentials the one that he had earlier created. It is the product of inspiration plus experience, and the quintessence of Schumann's nature.

Schumann wished this symphony to be played without breaks between the movements, all of which are associated by means of recurring themes. He avows no program and gives us no direct clue to his thoughts, but his purpose in the use of the repeated themes is manifestly for more reasons than those of structure. The motives have an emotional significance. They are as secret words coined by the poet for his Clara.

Some of these motives haunted Schumann for long after. The lovely brooding theme that opens the work is reincarnated in the symphonies that follow. Heard at the beginning of the D minor symphony in the strings, this idea reappears later as part of the romanza movement, and also in the trio of the scherzo. And there are other thematic inter-relations. In the introduction, following the brooding theme, is a restless auxiliary motive. A moment later this becomes the principal theme of the main body of the movement. Later the same idea occurs as transition from the scherzo to the finale, where, the tonality changing from minor to major, it becomes a salient motive of the last movement. By these means the symphony germinates from matter heard at the beginning.

In the first allegro movement the agitated figure carried over from the introduction tosses restlessly for many measures. The customary singing theme is not heard of until the free fantasia has been reached, and there is no "recapitulation." One mood, one thought, obsesses the composer's mind, and that is one of restless longing.

The next movement is the exquisite romance. The melody immediately announced by oboe and cello is said to be a Provençal song for which Schumann had intended a setting with guitar accompaniment. This melody merges into the flowing phrase made from the material of the introduction, which returns here in so natural a manner that the two motives seem parts of one idea. For contrast and elaboration there is a change from minor to major, with arabesques of the flowing theme by the solo violin. The movement, of subdued tint and pervasive melancholy, constitutes one of the loveliest passages in Schumann.

The scherzo commences with expected vigor, somewhat after the model of the same movement of the

First symphony, but what follows is quite different from the plan of the preceding work. It is an arrangement, in different rhythm, of the violin variation in the romanza. There is a wonderful bridge to the final movement—dying echoes of the scherzo theme, then, over tremolos of the strings and horn calls, the returning agitated phrase of the introduction. And now the mood changes. What had been despondency and protestation becomes the song of love triumphant. Rapid figures give place more and more frequently to lyric themes. The motive that had indicated heartache has become a herald of happiness and the pace quickens, as if the hastening lover could not speed fast enough, as if he sang as he sped.

•

Symphony in C major, Opus 61, numbered 2

I. Sostenuto assai; Allegro ma non troppo
II. Scherzo: Allegro vivace; Trio I, Trio II
III. Adagio espressivo
IV. Allegro molto vivace

The so-called Second symphony, really Schumann's Third, has melodic relations with the work that preceded it. Schumann was in poor spirits when he completed this score in 1845. He was physically ailing, mentally distressed. If there are any signs in the symphonies of the morbidness which turned in the last tragic years to insanity, they are here. The introduc-

tion, closely resembling that of the D minor symphony, is a troubled revery. The main movement,
while substantially worked out, is feverish. Toward
the end of the movement a horn figure already heard
in the introduction, and destined to reappear in later
movements, is sounded.

The scherzo continues in similar strain, a scherzo
brilliantly and in places curiously written. The first
part has a figure akin to the principal theme of the first
movement of the D minor symphony, but wilder in
mood, and the harmonies have more bite. There are
curious alternating rhythms in the trios, the first of
which, by a coincidence, is remindful of the figure
that opens the march movement of Tchaikovsky's
"Symphonie Pathétique." Some of the rhythmical
groupings must have puzzled Schumann's contemporaries. Here, too, is sensed a tragic undertone, and
again we hear the horn signal.

As a psychological document this symphony might
perhaps merit a closer examination than any of the
other four. For the music lover pure and simple the
slow movement alone, with its yearning melancholy,
would be worth the journey. The melody mounts in
pitch and in intensity to the inspired moment when
the violins, trilling passionately, descend by semi-
tones. There follows a passage of counterpoint, in
staccato notes, introduced for the sake of some contrast to the sustained song. It is almost laughably arti-
ficial—palpably a transparent device, unsuccessfully

employed. Not that it lacks plausibility. But this passage, truth to tell, could have been written by a good conservatory pupil. Our Schumann is for the moment far away! He is in bad case until after some academic fussing he gratefully resumes his song, and that song fairly transports us by its expression, so simple, so touching, so laden with his native appeal.

In the last movement—we are now speaking of the emotional issue—the composer in a measure recovers himself. Brilliant chords and scale passages precede a passionate theme given solo wind instruments over a throbbing accompaniment. The movement gains in momentum; the final sounding of the horn is as a pæan of victory. "In the finale," wrote Schumann to George Dietrich Otten, "I first began to feel myself; and indeed I was much better after I had finished the work. But otherwise, as I have said, it reminds me of a dark time." And elsewhere: "I sketched it when I was in a state of physical suffering; nay, I may say it was, so to speak, the resistance of the spirit which exercised a visible influence here, and through which I sought to contend with my bodily state. The first movement is full of this struggle and is very capricious and refractory." But when Jean Verhulst visited Schumann in 1845, the composer said that he had just finished a symphony; and he added, "I think it's a regular Jupiter"—alluding to Mozart's masterpiece. For the moment, at least, Schumann felt he had won his victory.

[123]

Symphony in E flat, Opus 97, ("Rhenish"), numbered 3

I. Lebhaft
II. Scherzo: Allegro vivace
III. Nicht schnell
IV. Feierlich
V. Lebhaft

It will be seen from the foregoing that Schumann's "Third" symphony was his last in actual conception. It is more frankly tone-painting than any of the others. Composed in 1850, this score is somewhat apart from the others. In a magnified way it is nearer related to Schumann's inimitable tone-pictures for the piano. The composer thought of the life, the festivities, and blue and gold of scenes along the banks of the Rhine. The symphony has the peculiarity of five movements, one of which was inspired by the spectacle of a religious ceremony witnessed in Cologne Cathedral. But Schumann struck out the one caption he had put over the fourth movement, which read, "In the character of the accompaniment of a solemn ceremony."

One trace of the Schumann of the earlier symphonies is here. It comes with the sudden appearance, in the midst of the festive tumult of the opening movement, of that haunting theme of the introduction of the D minor symphony! It is the voice of the dreamer, present in the midst of the thronging life of the people, of them and yet apart from them. It could well have borne the inscription which Schumann bestowed on one of his little piano pieces, "The Poet Speaks." For the rest, this opening movement of the "Rhenish" symphony is the most brightly colored page in Schumann's orchestral music. And again, as in a former work, he chooses to give nearly all his attention to his opening theme, which is sounded at once with great festivity, and without the formality of an introduction by the orchestra.

The next movement is a swinging dance measure, full of humor and naïveté—a true "Ländler," or country-dance of quieter days. The laughter and folk-like simplicity of the first part contrast with the lovely sentimentality of the trio, a passage of special felicity. No other composer, nor Schumann himself, ever said quite the same thing in music, in the same felicitous way.

The third movement, though not so designated, is another romanza, less melancholy than that of the D minor symphony, and very lovely. Schumann's art turns his longing sentimentalism to sheer poetry. In the fourth movement, the cathedral music, there is remarkable coloring due principally to the use of the trombones, and a special scheme of orchestration. All this is free tone-painting. The finale is an assembling of themes and moods, including a reminiscence of the cathedral music, which have gone before.

RICHARD WAGNER

1813–1883

I T IS more than half a century since the death of
Richard Wagner, one of the most significant, complex and fascinating figures in the history of music.
More has been written of Wagner than of any other
musician, which is inevitable, for no other musician
so permeated his art with the stuff of thought as well
as life. The amount of critical and biographical matter concerned with him is said to compare with the
bibliographies of Shakespeare and Napoleon.

A balanced estimate of Wagner, either as man or
musician, is still out of the question. Facts are accu-
mulating, but the data are incomplete and we are too
much in his shadow. Brilliant investigations have been
and are being conducted and almost every year adds
to the sum of Wagneriana. It will be years yet before
the returns are all in. But even if all material were
classified and available, we should still be far from a
just perspective of the artist Wagner. The reason for
this is that thus far in the history of music Wagner
has only background. There is no foreground to indi-

RICHARD WAGNER

cate his position relative to the present and future. There can be no scales in which to weigh him until another composer, as great as Wagner and with an equal sweep of vision, comes before us. This may not occur for centuries.

In the meantime we remain in the shadow of the colossus. As no other person in the world of music, Wagner bestrode his age and he dominates ours. There have been reactions against him, such as the impressionistic movement represented by the genius of Debussy. Since Debussy there have been smaller reactions. But how small they are in proportion, and how undeterminative, is shown by the very vehemence with which the disciples of new movements proclaim the passing of Wagner. They are little people, who picnic and chatter under the shadow of the mountain. They have forgotten the mountain, or think they have. Actually it conditions their whole existence. And it is so with Wagner and the relatively puny musical period which has followed him.

Between Bach and Beethoven in their epochs and Wagner in his is a profound fissure, not to be explained by a few years passing. The reason for this is the consciousness that animates Wagner's music. It represents more completely than the music of any other composer the coming of age of the intellectual musician and his meeting on equal terms with the modern man of experience and sensibility.

And how independently, with what complete originality, did Wagner express himself! He was a master of Bach counterpoint, but he escaped completely the formal consequences of the Bach procedure. Wagner's is the most flexible, expressive and magically eloquent counterpoint ever conceived. He realized that Beethoven, in his symphonies, had reached a consummation of the form. He heard Beethoven's passionate cry for liberty. He sensed new horizons for which Beethoven groped and toward which he fought.

Wagner did not attempt to follow in the steps of the master whom he so reverently studied—this in spite of the fact that the scores of the "Faust" overture and overtures and preludes to the operas make us regret keenly that Wagner in his mature years did not attempt a symphony. What he did was to incorporate the symphony in the music drama, thus giving the drama musical structure and intensity, and by union with drama and the projective power of poetic text enormously enrich and extend the boundaries of music.

It is music of higher nervous gear than had before been known; music astonishingly free, unchained, incandescent; of flaming depths and a myriad colors, yet, in spite of the frequent suggestion of the magician's cave, music of rugged force, masculinity and a fundamental kinship with nature. It is curious. Wagner, himself a Klingsor of his later years; Wagner, the unslakable sensualist—this same Wagner was a child of Nature, at home and at one with her in all her

moods and aspects. He heard and he echoed the wind
shrilling over the wild gray waste; the laughter and
anger of the storm, in the midst of which men and
gods contended on the mountain-top; or the flowing
of the Rhine or whispering of the forest. Everything
in the natural universe he knew and transfigured in
his music, a blend of primitiveness and unprecedented
subtlety and nervous tension; and lyrical intensity;
theatricalism and sensuality; and the loftiest idealism
and humanity and vision.

All this was in Wagner, whose life and character do
so much to explain his music. In the past even the
most subjective composers had lived somewhat apart
from their artistic creations. Beethoven, in deepest
sorrow, composed the Eighth symphony and many
other works as detached as that one from actual oc-
currences. Bach, whatever the melancholy and need
of his great and lonely soul, turned out compositions
of an everlasting beauty and symmetry, and did so as
systematically, to all appearance, as the carpenter
worked at his bench or the shoemaker at his last. Indeed, it may be said that of all composers Bach was
the one whose art most greatly and immeasurably
transcended him and his deepest conscious thinking.

But every word and note of Wagner's art-work
emanates directly and unmistakably from his personality. Everything he thought or participated in became material for his creations. In fact, the interplay
of experience and creation is one of the most signifi-

cant things that the life of Wagner illuminates for us. Sometimes, indeed more often than not, experience, with Wagner, followed instead of preceded the thought, the creative conception. Always the stuff of living was undergoing transformation in terms of art, and always the art was being given its impulse and color by living. This process lay at the bottom of Wagner's amazing capacity for development.

●

Overture to Th. Apel's drama, "Christoph Columbus"

The score of the "Christopher Columbus" overture of the youthful Richard Wagner, composed and performed in 1835, has had as many lives as the proverbial cat, and proved as immune to fortune's darts as Wagner himself in the days of his early trials and tribulations. It is bad music, being principally a youthful adulteration of Meyerbeer and Weber. It was composed while Wagner, in the first year of his professional career, was learning his business as conductor of a one-horse opera company in Magdeburg, and tempestuously wooing the young actress, Minna Planer. And yet this overture, which sprawls like a puppy on weak legs, has a certain clear expressive purpose, and shows already Wagner's temperament and the dramatic direction of his genius.

There appeared one day at Magdeburg a friend of

Wagner's, Guido Theodore Apel, poet, dramatist and amateur musician, and a young man of some means, with a play, "Christopher Columbus," which he desired to have mounted in Wagner's theater and for which Wagner agreed to write incidental music in the form of an overture, chorus and orchestral epilogue.

At the first performance the overture "astonished everyone and was tumultuously applauded." It was repeated several times by request. The drama was never given again, but Apel had lived to see a play of his own performed on the stage and he was grateful to Wagner. Upon him he bestowed a gold signet ring which proved pawnable and was soon put to that use by the future master of music drama. When, four years later, Wagner fled from his creditors to Paris, he took the overture with him. There were at least two performances in the French capital. Wagner then sent the score to that singular being, half-musician and half-mountebank, Louis Antoine Jullien, then conducting orchestral concerts in London and succeeding by showmanship where others had failed by honester means. Jullien rejected the overture, which was shortsighted of him, for he toured America, that "land of barbarians," in the Fifties with an orchestra that caused ladies to faint when it performed, with the aid of real firemen, flames, whistles and hose, and breaking glass, the "Firemen's Quadrille". And in that year—1853—a "Christopher Columbus" overture by Richard Wagner, then rapidly advancing in reputation, would have been a splendid card. But we cannot foresee the future! When the overture was returned to him, Wagner was unable to pay the cartage, and the bundle was returned to the warehouse. A friend of Wagner's tried later to recover the score, but the last surviving member of the carting company had died, and there was no trace of the music. Years were to pass before it turned up. Then it was discovered on one of the second-hand book-stalls that line the bank of the Seine, in Paris in 1889, the year of the Paris Exposition, by an impecunious music student, Andrew de Ternant, who could not pay the *forty centimes* asked for the manuscript. De Ternant begged the old woman who attended the stall to lay the music aside and hold it for him a few days. She did not keep her promise. When he returned with his eight cents she had sold the score to a person described as a young lady, probably an Englishwoman, in spectacles. At last the score materialized in London. It was performed by Henry Wood in 1905 and was finally published in 1907. Wagner would have given much if in 1835 there had been the solicitude to perform anything bearing his name that there is today. The principal value of the "Christopher Columbus" overture is documentary. Who could believe that the composer of this flimsy stuff would one day pen the preludes to "Tristan und Isolde" and "Die Meistersinger"?

Overture to "The Flying Dutchman"

"The Flying Dutchman," composed in 1841 and produced in 1843, was the first opera in which Wagner realized something of his new ideas of music drama. In several respects this overture is autobiographical. Its circumstantial background is Wagner's flight from his creditors in 1839, from Riga to Paris via London, and the terrific weather that his ship encountered on the North Sea. The boat was small, and the trip lasted a fantastic number of days. The legendary *Dutchman* himself had hardly a worse time of it rounding Cape Horn. There was a moment of complete terror, when Minna, now Wagner's wife, begged the composer to tie him to her with a rope, that they might drown together. The ship sought refuge in a Norwegian fjord. Through the wind and mist the men on shore and the sailors called to each other, and this call, reshaped by Wagner's genius, became the sailors' chorus of the opera. But the triumphant creation in the overture, one which in itself would proclaim Wagner's greatness, is the *Dutchman's* motive which sounds so eerily when it is flung out by the horns against the empty fifths of the strings at the beginning of the overture. To this motive Wagner adds, later on, the prayerlike theme of *Senta,* the maiden who at the last gives her life for the *Dutchman's* salvation; subsidiary motives from the opera, such as the Spinning Song of *Senta's* maidens, which seems to be heard amid the skirling of the elements, and the chorus of sailors; and, to complete the musical synthesis of the dramatic developments, the motive of redemption, heard as *Senta* throws herself into the sea.

The peroration of the overture, preceded by a pause and an upward rush of the strings, summarizes dramatically the themes of *Senta,* of her sacrifice, and the motive, now in the major key, of the redeemed mariner.[1] Wagner's overture is a seascape; it is to the ocean what Weber's "Freischütz" overture is to the forest. But Weber's forest is a German forest, a woodland home of myth and folklore. Wagner's ocean is the vast deep, a tossing waste of wind and spume and cloud wrack. The texture of Wagner's music is coarser and more sensational than Weber's, and has the grander sweep. Wagner is at home with storm and sea. In the figure of the *Dutchman* doomed, unless he should find the loving and rescuing woman, to sail the seas forever, he saw himself, alone and adrift in a hostile, uncomprehending world, seeking beauty and the realization of his genius.

But it is of interest, especially in view of Cosima Wagner's later attempts to minimize the influence of Wagner's first wife, that in the first draft of the libretto of "The Flying Dutchman" the heroine, now named *Senta,* was called *Minna.*

[1] The resemblance in treatment between this conclusion and that of the "Freischütz" overture, plainly its model, is obvious.

Overture and Bacchanale from "Tannhäuser"

The overture and Bacchanale from "Tannhäuser" combine characteristics of Wagner's earlier period with those of his mature years. "Tannhäuser" was composed in 1845. In 1861 it was revised. The overture and opening scene of the opera were joined together and the Bacchanale and scene with Venus greatly extended for the Paris première of the work; that première which became a historical scandal through the opposition of the Jockey Club. The story is now well known: how a group of snobs and idlers demanded a ballet in the second act of the opera, where there was dramatically no occasion for one; how Wagner refused utterly to spoil his score for the sake of such cattle, but attempted a compromise by putting the ballet in the first act; how the precious *jeunesse dorée* of the boulevards and their petted favorites of the ballet, unsatisfied by this arrangement, plotted and succeeded in catcalling the opera off the stage. But even such catastrophes have their value. The upshot of the Paris première was for the great gain of posterity, since Wagner rewrote and extended many pages of his score with the knowledge he had gained in later operas up to "Tristan und Isolde," and the result is a combination of the early faith and fervors of the overture with the inspiration and authority of Wagner at the height of his powers. (Incidentally, when the Germans marched into Paris after the French débâcle of 1870, its military bands played the march from "Tannhäuser!")

Although the end of the overture is altered to merge it with the Bacchanale, this occasion may be taken to consider the two scores by themselves, as well as the form in which they are combined. Let us first take the overture. It is in three great parts. The first is the proclamation of the celebrated hymn, the "Pilgrims' Chorus," announced by wind instruments and horns, then by the trombones against brilliant and dramatic ornamentation of the strings, ornamentation which proves later to have a special significance. The second part is the music of the Venusberg, announced by a leaping figure for the violas, flutes and oboes; a bacchanalian theme, called by some industrious German commentators "drunkenness of the Horselberg"—the Venus-mountain. It includes the music of *Tannhäuser's* hymn to Venus, played by the strings, and a song of the solo clarinet—the voice of Venus herself; this whole passage with its several themes being mighty and blazing tonal evocation of what Baudelaire, an arrant Wagnerian, called "the true, the terrible, the universal Venus." "Venus"— Wagner is now speaking—bears *Tannhäuser* "where no step dare tread, to the realm of Being-no-more— weaving forgetfulness, loss of self in the sensual ecstasy." The third part is redemption. There is a remarkable transformation by means of which the swirling figure of the Venusberg revels becomes, grad-

ually, the brilliant ornamentation of the violins heard
as corollary of the trombones' chant of the "Pilgrims'
Chorus," and that chorus, hymned by the whole orchestra—token of *Tannhäuser's* deliverance and salvation—brings the overture to an end. Here are Wagner's words descriptive of the imaginary situation, as
also of the conclusion of his drama: "Dawn begins to
break. From afar is heard again the Pilgrims' chant.
As the chant draws near, closer yet and closer, as the
day drives farther back the night, that whir and
soughing of the air—which had erstwhile sounded
like the eerie cries of souls condemned—now rises to
ever gladder waves; so that when the sun ascends at
last in splendor, and the Pilgrims' chant proclaiming
in ecstasy to the world that to all that lives and moves
thereon salvation is won, this wave itself swells out
the tidings of sublimest joy. 'Tis the carol of the
Venusberg redeemed from the curse of impiousness,
this cry we hear amid the hymn of God. So wells and
leaps each pulse of life in chorus of Redemption; and
both dissevered elements, both soul and senses, God
and nature, unite in the atoning kiss of hallowed
love."

So much for the overture, which, by itself, figures
so often and effectively on concert programs. The
concert arrangement of overture and Bacchanale al-
ters and greatly extends this material. Wagner takes
the Venusberg music as his point of departure, treat-
ing it with a wealth of color and intensity of which

he had not earlier been capable. The rising curtain (as the composer conceived the spectacle) discovers the retreats of the Horselberg—bacchantic revelry, dances of nymphs, fauns and satyrs, allegorical groups representing the abduction of Europa and Leda and the swan, and, to the last faint and exquisite sounds, the bosky retreats of the sirens of Venus. In this music there is much new material, and a style wholly superior in flexibility, color and dramatic incisiveness to anything that has preceded. It is a particularly illuminating example of the growth of a genius. Wagner wrote "Tannhäuser," says Ernest Newman, "in a state of burning exaltation," and fear that he would die before his task was completed. The opera was an "autobiographical revelation of his own secret sorrow and despair," his disgust with the sensual and material world, his craving for the Ideal. "Thus the music juxtaposes the religious song and the voluptuous song" and "at last, in overture and opera, these songs become one, a hymn of redemption, of homage to God and nature."

•

Prelude to "Lohengrin"

The Prelude to "Lohengrin" (composed in 1848 and produced in 1850) is musically symbolic of the descent of the Holy Grail, its presentation to those who supplicate and adore, and the return of the sacred vessel to its home in the heavens. Wagner's somewhat turgid and involved phraseology is best conveyed to English readers in Mr. Newman's concise translation:

"Out of the clear blue ether of the sky there seems to condense a wonderful, yet at first hardly percept- ible vision; and out of this there gradually emerges, ever more and more clearly, an angel host bearing in its midst the sacred Grail. As it approaches earth it pours out exquisite odors, like streams of gold, rav- ishing the senses of the beholder. The glory of the vision grows and grows, until it seems as if the rap- ture must be shattered and dispersed by the very ve- hemence of its own expansion. The vision draws nearer, and the climax is revealed in all its glorious reality, radiating fiery beams and shaking the soul with emotion. The beholder sinks on his knees in adoring self-annihilation. The Grail pours out its light on him like a benediction, and consecrates him to its service; then the flames gradually die away, and the angel host soars up again to the ethereal heights in tender joy, having made pure once more the hearts of men by the sacred blessings of the Grail."

This "Lohengrin" Prelude is a miracle of inspira- tion and atmosphere. Only the Prelude to "Tristan und Isolde" is more subtly contrived, and the accents of "Tristan" are dark and sultry with passion, whereas this strain is radiant as the skies. It is wholly mysterious, a miraculous birth. There is a life without beginning or end, once the ethereal harmonics of two violin

desks have been sounded, to the musical phrases which
are elements of a single thought. The parts of this
strangely integrated conception weave together as
the vision of the Grail descends. What was at first
but mystical radiance becomes a glowing harmony
that permeates the whole atmosphere, until, with a
glory and flash of color which are almost visual, the
trombones proclaim the unveiling of the sacred vessel
to the eyes of man. Thereafter the instruments are
gradually withdrawn as the Grail ascends and disappears in the sky whence it came. This score reverses
the customary order of musical climax. Usually music
rises in pitch as it rises in intensity. Here the lowest
pitch is the moment for a climax of supreme majesty.
Notice, also, how Wagner, as one might say, protects
and encases his musical Grail in tone of its own stuff,
diffused all about it. As the vessel never touches the
earth, so this music seems to be suspended, without
contacts, in the atmosphere. Wagner never surpassed
the originality and delicacy of these pages of orchestration. If he had only this flash of consummate genius to
his credit he would be one of the greatest composers.

•

Prelude and Love-Death from "Tristan und Isolde"

The Prelude to "Tristan und Isolde" (completed
1859, produced 1865), leads in the original score di-

rectly into the first act of the opera. In the concert version it is often linked with the "Liebestod" of the final pages of the music-drama. Wagner's concept here is that of the thwarted passion to which life could only offer insuperable obstacles, for which the night was sanctuary and the day destruction, and death the only possible consummation. The supreme ecstasy and ultimate tragedy appeared to him inseparable, and so from the first measure of the "Tristan" Prelude we feel the accents not merely of superhuman longing but inevitable doom. This is the key to the Prelude and even to the ecstatic music of *Isolde's* transfiguration. In this Prelude are no fewer than seven motives, that of death being intimately bound with that of love, the two motives intertwining, as the legend says the rose and laurel entwine above the graves of *Tristan* and *Isolde*. These musical and emotional strands are so closely combined that they seem to grow from each other. They fuse at the catastrophic climax when the music of cruel desire and inexorable fate has intensified to the point where Wagner precipitates every agency of the orchestra in a cry of despair. Then the music falls back upon itself, and low tones of the strings prepare the point of modulation to the "Liebestod." From the depths of the orchestra rises a phrase already heard in the love duet of the second act, and the music mounts, shaking out its wings, said George Moore, as the souls of the lovers disappear over the horizon. We can perceive the genesis of this conception far back in the crude though powerful beginnings of "The Flying Dutchman."

•

Prelude to "Die Meistersinger"

A recital of Wagner's deeds in music becomes an unending tale of marvel. Wagner had conceived the plan of "Die Meistersinger" (completed in 1867, produced 1868) very early, as early as or even earlier than "Lohengrin." But, though some have claimed that he made early sketches for the quintet from the last act of "Die Meistersinger," he apparently did not set himself definitely to its composition till the middle of March, 1862. He was, as usual, terrifically in debt, but had settled himself comfortably in Biebrich, in rooms that looked out upon a garden and a flowing river, and the creative mood, as he had hoped it would, descended upon him. In his autobiography he tells us that "As from the balcony of my flat, in a sunset of great splendor, I gazed upon the magnificent spectacle of 'golden' Mayence, with the majestic Rhine flooding its outskirts in a glory of light, the Prelude to my Meistersinger again suddenly made its presence closely and distinctly felt in my soul. Once before had I seen it rise before me out of a lake of sorrow, like some distant mirage. I wrote down the prelude exactly as it appears today in the score, containing the clear outlines of the leading themes of the whole drama. I proceeded at once to continue the composition, intending to allow the remaining scenes to follow in due succession."

We must consider for a moment the basic dramatic motives of the opera if we are to grasp fully the meaning of this Prelude. The principal characters in the plot are *Walther von Stolzing*, poet and knight; *Eva*, daughter of a rich burgher of old-time Nuremberg, whom *Walther* loves, but whose hand he can win only by proving his genius in song; *Hans Sachs*, the famous cobbler and Mastersinger, who personifies the wisdom of experience and sacrifice, and the great-heartedness of the people; and *Beckmesser*, the crabbed clerk, pedant and theoretician, who expects by virtue of his hollow learning and pretense to win *Eva* for himself. At last *Beckmesser* and *Walther* are pitted against each other in a contest of song, when *Walther's* genius, youth and love put the now ridiculous *Beckmesser* to flight. *Walther* is acclaimed a Mastersinger; *Eva* is given to him as his bride; the populace enthusiastically salute the poet and the noble *Sachs*.

Walther, of course, is Wagner himself. *Beckmesser* is prototype of Wagner's antagonists among the critics. *Hans Sachs* is the virtue and wisdom of the people, prompt to recognize the creative artist and find expression in him. The final moral is that the greatest genius must have its roots deep down in the soil of the race that gave it birth, and that the aristocracy of genius can in turn raise the people to new levels of beauty and understanding.

The Prelude begins with the first of the two "Meistersinger" themes, a splendid pompous march emblematic of that famous sixteenth-century guild of musician-tradesmen and merchants who practiced art industriously, even though they tended to conventionalize it, and gave poetry and music official importance in the lives of the people. The march theme is followed by phrases that relate to *Walther's* Prize Song and his love for *Eva*. This leads to the second "Meistersinger" theme, also in march rhythm, and, if anything, more weighty than the first. You are to see them, these Mastersingers, as they wend their way to the banks of the river to hold the contest of song— the noble *Sachs*, the majestical *Pogner*, the mincing *Beckmesser*, clad in rich fabrics and colors, mighty in the consciousness of their own pith and prosperity and worth. Banners fly, the people dance and cheer and crane their necks as the leading citizens of the free and imperial city of the olden time pass by. This second march theme, which Wagner is said to have taken from the "Crowned tone" of Heinrich Mügling, is extended with music heard in the festive concluding scenes, the music of the crowd and the holiday. A short, impetuous phrase given the strings speaks of the love of *Walther* and *Eva*, and the basic motive of *Walther's* Prize Song is developed by the orchestra.

This is the substance of the first part of the Prelude, which propounds all its musical material. The second part comes with the fugal caricature of the "Meistersinger" theme, combined with a motive heard when the populace makes fun of *Beckmesser* in the last act. The fugue is cackled by the wind instruments, with humorous asides by trilling strings and other similar effects. Thus Wagner makes fun of the pedantry of the Beckmessers. The progress of the fugue is hotly contested, from time to time, by the warm and impetuous motive of *Walther* and *Eva*. The two motives oppose each other with increasing obstinacy, which brings the fugue to a climax.

The third part of the Prelude begins when the brasses thunder out in its full grandeur the first "Meistersinger" theme, which disperses the fussy counterpoint, while an exultant phrase wreathes the motive of the sturdy march. Now occurs that sheer explosion of genius, the peroration of the "Meistersinger" Prelude. Three themes and a fragment of a fourth are heard at the same time, as though it were impossible to keep them apart and oblige each one to wait its turn. Softly, in the basses, walks along the theme of the Mastersingers. Above sings the Prize Song of *Walther*. In between may be heard the fanfares of the second "Meistersinger" motive, and across the strings flits a motive associated with *Beckmesser*. The glorious hubbub grows, the music swells with lustiness and festivity to the final proclamation, with

[145]

all possible orchestral brilliancy, of the "Meister-singer" music.

•

"Siegfried Idyll"

The late Siegfried Wagner, inheritor of Bayreuth, was born to Richard Wagner and Cosima in 1869. Wagner, then at the height of his artistic powers, was deeply involved in the tangled skein of his last and consummative love affair and the completion of his opera "Siegfried." Cosima, as Wagner wrote a friend, had "defied every disapprobation and taken upon herself every condemnation. She has borne to me a wonderfully beautiful and vigorous boy, whom I could boldly call 'Siegfried'; he is now growing, together with my work, and gives me a new long life which has at last attained a meaning." In 1870, after Cosima had secured her divorce from von Bülow and become Wagner's wife, the composer wrote his friend Prager that his house was full of children, those of his wife by her former marriage, and of his joy in his own son, "whom I dare to call Siegfried Richard Wagner. Now think what I must feel, that this at last has fallen to my share. I am fifty-seven years old." This was the year of the composition of the "Siegfried Idyll."

If Cosima, as a lately published biography shows, suffered bitter hours of remorse for her abandonment of von Bülow ("The serpent lies hidden in paradise, it lurks in my heart, while all around is happiness, so radiant and beautiful. Let us pray—destiny is deepest sorrow and supreme happiness"); if she prayed, as her diary would indicate, that all the agonies she had suffered or caused were justified by her devotion to Wagner, the "Siegfried Idyll" must almost have affected her as a sign of pardon.

It was arranged that the performance should be a complete surprise to Cosima. She was born on a Christmas Day. The "Idyll" was completed in November of 1870. Wagner handed the score to Hans Richter, the conductor, early in December. Richter copied the music and rehearsed the orchestra, at Zurich, and when the time came took part in the performance. Early in the morning of Christmas, 1870, the musicians assembled, tuned instruments in the kitchen and quietly mounted the narrow stairs. There they grouped themselves, Wagner at their head and out of sight of the 'cello and double-bass players, who formed the lowest rank.

At precisely seven-thirty in the morning the performance began. Cosima, in the diary she left her children, says: "I can give you no idea, my children, about this day, nor about my feelings. I shall only tell you quite barely what happened: As I awoke, my ear caught a sound, which swelled fuller and fuller; no longer could I imagine myself to be dreaming: music was sounding, and such music! When it died away, Richard came into my room with the children and offered me the score of the symphonic birthday poem. I was in tears, but so were all the rest of the household. Richard had arranged his orchestra on the staircase, and thus was our Triebschen consecrated forever."

In the early morning Wagner heard Cosima's servant, Vreneli, the good angel of the house, cry, "Ein sohn ist da." Siegfried was born while the rising sun turned into a blaze of the color of the orange wallpaper outside Cosima's room, a bird sang, and chiming bells sounded over the Lake of Lucerne. When Wagner heard the same bird later at sunset, he called it Siegfried's bird. On the title-page of his manuscript he wrote, "Triebschen Idyll [Triebschen was later changed to Siegfried], with Fidi's bird-song and orange sunrise, as symphonic birthday greeting from Richard to Cosima."

Wagner wrote a dedication to his wife. All the themes in this composition except one come from the opera "Siegfried." The added theme is the folksong "Schlaf, mein Kind." The first theme, which has likewise the character of a lullaby, is from the scene of *Brünnhilde's* awakening in the third act. Later a flute plays the motive of *Brünnhilde's* slumber, first heard in "Die Walküre." One of the most salient motives of the score, often repeated, is a descending phrase of two notes, answered by triplet pulsations of the wind instruments. This also comes from the love scene in "Siegfried." After considerable development of these

[148]

ideas, *Siegfried's* horn-call, the call of the hero who knew not fear, is heard. The song of the bird in the forest scene is added by flute and clarinet. After prolonged trills of the instruments comes a last phrase from the opera, the song of *Siegfried*, "Ein herrlich Gewassertragt wogt vor mir." The "Idyll" is a free rhapsody on these themes, and there is no better example of the flexibility and emotional import of Wagner's music than the way in which they are treated, which is entirely different from anything in the opera from which they come.

CÉSAR FRANCK

1822–1890

Symphony in D minor

   I.   Lento—Allegro non troppo
  II.   Allegretto
 III.   Allegro non troppo

THE dark, glowing, mystical symphony of César Franck is constantly suggestive of the organ on which he was wont to improvise in the loft of Ste. Clotilde's in Paris. Franck was a Belgian, a poor music-teacher in Paris, one of the meek whose praises are sung in the "Beatitudes" which he set to music. He had lived a hard youth at the hands of a father whose intention it was to exploit his precocious musical talent; for Franck, at an early age, could play the piano brilliantly. Because of this exploitation, and other repressive circumstances, Franck was long in reaching his creative maturity. As a young, industrious and not over-fortunate musician he married a wife whom he came to fear, and the wedding party climbed over the barricades of the Commune. In an age of social corruption and vitiated public taste, a period of cynical materialism, Franck pursued his way, and his music falls upon the ear like the still small voice of vision and faith. He never arrogated virtue to himself, but composed, in his most prosperous years, two hours in the early morning, before he began to trot around Paris giving lessons, and in the evening gathered about him a group of young disciples which came to include some of the leading composers of modern France. By the self-seeking, Franck was ignored; and when he died, as the result of a street accident, professors of the Conservatoire where he taught were pointedly absent from the obsequies. When his symphony was first performed in 1888 it was ridiculed by eminent authorities and coldly received by the public. But when Franck was asked about it, according to Vincent d'Indy, his pupil and biographer, his face glowed and he answered happily, "Oh, it sounded well, just as I thought it would."

Franck has been called a composer without the dramatic spirit. What is meant is probably his complete innocence of theatricalism. His symphony is the inner drama of doubt and triumph. His is the cry of the man who supplicates: "Lord, I believe; help thou my unbelief."

The first theme (1) of the symphony, announced by the basses and 'cellos, is the root of many developments, and of a cyclic treatment of thematic material which develops variously in different movements, in a manner peculiarly Franck's.

The opening of this symphony could be the scene of the unveiling of the Grail. It is profoundly meditative and tender.

There is something indescribably rich, shadowy and mystical in the shifting harmonies that merge chromatically, one into another, in the introduction, and the tremulous figures of the strings that have the shadow and mystery of cathedral arches. After repetition of this sombre and majestic introduction come more impassioned pages and the addition of a completing phrase to the first theme (2). A lyrical second theme (3), tender and sensuous, is given the strings, with an answer from the 'cellos in free imitation. The solo trumpet has a majestic motive (4) like the swinging of the censer. This trumpet phrase, as also the theme of the opening, is carried over into other movements. The first movement of the symphony has the customary divisions—the statement of the themes, their development (5), and restatement. When the moment for restatement comes it does so with a stern magnificence that is utterly Gothic, the passage being given principally to the brass, in "imitation," in the canonic manner (6). Again the strings carry upward their supplication. The last measures of this movement, after a peculiarly agitated development, present once more the initial motive of three notes, carved as if from granite by the reverberant orchestra. It is the composer's signature, "César Franck," and the capstone of the movement.

The second movement is a religious meditation. Formally it combines elements of the slow movement and scherzo. It opens, after chromatic harmonies of harp and strings, with a song of the English horn that only Franck could have conceived (7). In repetition a warm counter-phrase of the 'cellos is set against it. Later there are fantastical scherzo figures for the strings (8). Then the song of the English horn and the flickering string figures combine. A new theme, over the accompaniment of the strings, is given the clarinet (9). Toward the end of the movement comes one of the most touching passages in the symphony, when the wind choir responds with chorale-like phrases to the melody of the violins (10). I know little in music so naïve and tender—a little conversation of Franck, fearless as a child, and his God.

The finale of this symphony is not only dramatic, but almost spectacular in certain of its pages. The color is golden. The shadows have gone. The opening is jubilant, quivering with light. A joyous melody is played by the violoncellos (11). Later, at first softly and then with commanding brilliancy, the brasses intone the song of the warrior of the faith (12). There are various contrasting episodes, some of them subdued and self-questioning. But this is not for long. Radiant decorations of tone are flung about the themes. Motives from the preceding movements return. The English horn theme of the second movement appears first under a "triplet" figuration (13); reappearing, it is flung out with the full power and splendor of the orchestra (14). Toward the end the trumpet motive of the first movement is discoursed

[153]

by woodwinds, then by strings in a low register, then whispered by the violins high up over a deep gulf of tone (15), the harmonies for the low strings being so spaced as to remind one of similar great depths in the instrumentation of Beethoven. There is an instant when the symphony hangs between heaven and earth, before it begins to ascend, with sweeping harps and horn-calls from the promised land. The calls are repeated in rising sequences. In answer, motives previously heard assemble (18), as the just and the unjust, the quick and the dead, might assemble and pass before the throne. At last the higher brass instruments send forth stabs of light, like that which lances from the sky in old Italian religious pictures.

This symphony has not Beethoven's intensiveness, and it is no longer an expression of modernism. But its pure, naïve and passionate spirit will for a long time search the hearts of men.

Quotations from Strauss's 'Till Eulenspiegel'

ANTON BRUCKNER

1824–1896

Symphony No. 7, in E major

I. Allegro moderato
II. Adagio: Sehr feierlich und langsam
III. Scherzo: Sehr schnell; Trio: Etwas langsamer
IV. Finale: Bewegt, doch nicht schnell

THE question of the value of Bruckner's symphonies has divided musical opinion ever since these symphonies were composed. Frequent post-mortems have been conducted in their honor, but these have proved immature. The Bruckner symphonies have a way of remaining in the repertory. It is something of a testimonial to him that hour-long compositions, without cuts, by a composer who remains outside the pale of the conversationally entertaining, continue to be heard and acclaimed by at least considerable elements of modern audiences. The Bruckner symphonies are nine in number, and they have different characteristics within the confines of their immense but by no means entirely cohesive structures. The music is prevailingly Wagnerian in texture, and also powerfully impregnated with the spirit of the German chorale. They are tremendous fragments rather than completed monuments. Because of their musical and spiritual essence they are precious. Where Franck was

[162]

Belgian, Bruckner was German in his mysticism, without Franck's clarity and lucidity of thought, or subtlety in modulation.

We need not deny that the Seventh symphony, like all Bruckner's symphonic conceptions, would gain in clarity and effectiveness if it lasted forty instead of sixty minutes. In addition, it is uneven and in places disjointed. At one moment Bruckner prophesies like John of Patmos; at the next he may lose the thread of his discourse. Nevertheless, his music is that of heavenly spaces.

Bruckner, whose behavior, at times, was that of a humble and subservient peasant, had his convictions, which he expressed in his inimitable way. One day he said to a friend: "I think that if Beethoven were alive, and I should go to him with my Seventh symphony and say, 'Here, Mr. Beethoven, this is not so bad, this Seventh, as certain gentlemen would make out,'—I think he would take me by the hand and say, 'My dear Bruckner, never mind, I had no better luck; and the same men who hold me against you even now do not understand my last quartets, although they act as if they understood them.' Then I'd say, 'Excuse me, Mr. van Beethoven, that I have gone beyond you in freedom of form, but I think a true artist should make his own forms and stick by them.' " And stick by them Bruckner did.

Of the four movements of the Seventh symphony the slow movement is the most famous. It has had especial attention because of a public belief, which seems misleading on the face of the actual evidence, that the composer intended the movement as a dirge in memory of Richard Wagner. This story has been given credence by Bruckner himself, who once wrote the conductor Felix Mottl, of the slow movement, "Please take a very slow and solemn tempo. At the close, in the Dirge (in memory of the death of the Master), think of our ideal," and in scoring this passage Bruckner used the tubas which Wagner had employed with such magnificent effect in operas of the "Ring of the Nibelungs," and which had made a sensation in Bayreuth. But the fact is that the letter to Mottl was written in 1885; that Wagner died in 1883; and that, according to the best evidence, the slow movement of the symphony was completed by Bruckner in 1882, five months before Wagner's death. Bruckner said nothing about Wagner when the symphony was first performed, under Nikisch, in his presence. In 1900, eight years later, he wrote Mottl: "At one time I came home and was very sad; I thought to myself, it is impossible that the Master can live for a long time; and then the Adagio in C sharp minor came into my head." One wonders. Bruckner was preëminently an honest and simple man, and yet all of us have ways of persuading ourselves that at a certain time we thought this or that, or did something from a different motive than actually animated us at the moment. It matters little what circumstances

[164]

led to the composition of the Adagio, any more than it matters that Beethoven had Napoleon in mind when he began to write the "Eroica" symphony. Bruckner's epical funeral march, like Beethoven's, is of universal meaning. To narrow its significance is to make it smaller and less profound. Beethoven, Bruckner—and how many others!—have suffered from conceptions of little men, prone to find in the expressions of great souls something that reflected the limitations of themselves!

Think of Bruckner's life. Like Schubert, he was one of a large and poor Austrian family, of humble birth and miserable circumstances. In his youth, teaching school, and playing the organ for seventy-five cents a month, he nearly starved. He tried to eke out a living by fiddling for dances and weddings. The musical training he needed as composer was denied him till comparatively late. When he was thirty-seven he was studying theory and orchestration, and was over forty when he composed his first symphony. Nevertheless, when he was examined for his skill in counterpoint by a committee of three, the conductor Anton Herbeck—the same who discovered the score of Schubert's "Unfinished" symphony—said, "It is he who should examine us"; and Bruckner lived to teach theory and composition and lecture on these and other subjects at the Vienna Conservatory of Music. A dreamer, he stumbled awkwardly, with groping hands and shining face toward God.

JOHANNES BRAHMS

1833–1897

Symphony No. 1, in C minor, Opus 68

I. Un poco sostenuto; Allegro
II. Andante sostenuto
III. Un poco allegretto e grazioso
IV. Adagio; Piú andante; Allegro non troppo, ma con brio

BRAHMS waited ten years longer than Beethoven did to issue a first symphony, and was undoubtedly hesitant because of his awe of the composer of the Nine. In the interval of the seventy-six years that elapsed between the two works, Brahms had opportunity to benefit by the colossal strides of Beethoven himself and by immense technical advances in composition and orchestration. Another thing: to write a symphony in 1876 was considerably more of a responsibility than to undertake one in 1800. In 1800 the symphony was a comparatively modest affair. Composers turned them out in batches, as we have had opportunity to observe. But with the appearance of the "Eroica" symphony of Beethoven in 1804 all that was changed. The symphonic form was now the repository of the grandest musical and emotional conceptions. When Schumann, as a critic, discovered Brahms, and revealed him to the world in a famous

[166]

article, he spoke of him as a creative artist who sprang forth fully armed, like Minerva from the head of Jove; and that, thanks to Brahms's patience, structural power and depth of meaning, holds true of the C minor symphony. It is monumental in proportions and epical in spirit, complex in structure, essentially dramatic as Beethoven's Fifth symphony is dramatic, and, incidentally, concerned with the same theme.

The first movement is storm and stress; everything in it is tremendous, concentrated, richly developed and packed together with great strength and a bardic power of utterance. The opening is one of the greatest pages of modern orchestral music, born of mist and storm and towering heights. The striving phrase heard over the pounding drums is the basic motive of the symphony, reappearing in many different guises in the following movements. It recurs like a question in measures of the slow movement. It ponders, dark-visaged and Faust-like, in the opening measures of the introduction of the finale, before the orchestral sky clears and Brahms's horn brings promise of salvation. There are pages in the first movement when it is as if the earth were in travail. There are hammer-blows of fate, and at the end of the movement a calmer mood, a suggestion, at least, of a band of light at the edge of a tempestuous sky.

From all this turmoil the slow movement is remote, although its exaltations are haunted by questionings and agitations of the spirit. The third movement is not a minuet or a scherzo, but an allegretto—not a dance but a walk through nature; not laughter but a smile tinged with melancholy, and a departure, original with Brahms, from the customary symphonic form. In this symphony the last movement as well as the first has an introduction, and the second introduction is perhaps Brahms's boldest imaginative flight. It begins in a vein of somber reverie. Curious pizzicato passages of the strings and savage outbursts of the full orchestra prelude the passage where the trilling strings shimmer out like the opening of the heavens, and the horn calls as from above. There have been various explanations of this dramatic passage, of the origin of the horn motive,[1] and its meaning. The

[1] It is quoted in notation in a letter from Brahms to Clara Schumann, dated September 12, 1868 ("Letters of Brahms and Clara Schumann," edited by Dr. Berthold Litzmann. English edition by Longmans, Green & Company, 1927). Brahms, then in the mountains, sends Clara, with whom he apparently has had a tiff, a birthday greeting. Clara's birthday being the 13th, his letter accompanies a gift and contains in notation the theme incorporated eight years later in the symphony. Under the theme Brahms has written six words: "Thus blew the Alpine horn today." The melody, with one slight rhythmical variation, is identic in note, measure and key with the horn theme of the finale of the C minor symphony. In the letter a fragment of sentimental peasant verse is fitted to it.

> "Hoch auf'm Berg, tief im Tal,
> Grüss ich Dich, viel tausendmal."

Did the verse and the melody originally belong together? Probably not. Variants of the verse are to be found in collections of German folk-poetry, such as

> "Hoch auf'm Berg und tief im Thal
> Soll ich denn um Dich trauren wohl überall?"

[168]

association with mountain scenery is inescapable, and
would immediately occur to us, even if we knew
nothing of the theme's beginnings. But there is a far
deeper significance, though one that a modern generation might pooh-pooh. It is that of faith. The prophetic
motto, following after dark mystery and brooding,

In Wyss's "Collection of Swiss Cowherd Melodies and Folksongs" (1826) a variant of these lines is fitted to another air not
in the least resembling the one under discussion, and far more
conventional. But in no collection of folk-music have I been able
to discover the original of Brahms's melody.

It is a striking coincidence that the first four measures of the
horn theme are identic with those of one of the quarters of what
are now popularly known as the Westminster chimes. These
chimes were copied by the Houses of Parliament in London from
the chimes of St. Mary's Church at Cambridge University. They
are believed to have been arranged by Dr. William Crotch, and
they were placed in the tower of St. Mary's in 1793–94. Brahms
had completed three movements of his First symphony when
Cambridge invited him to visit the university and accept the
honorary degree of Doctor of Music. This was in May, 1876. The
finale of the symphony, in which the horn theme makes its first
appearance, was not finished till the September following. Brahms
did not accept the Doctor's degree, for he was reluctant to go to
England, and the degree could not be conferred *in absentia*. But
in the following year, March 8, 1877, Brahms sent the score of
the First symphony to be conducted by Joachim at Cambridge,
in token of appreciation of the honor which had been proffered
him. The performance was accompanied by a dramatic incident
when "the audience in the Guild-hall heard the horn phrase answered, as it seemed, by the chimes of St. Mary's Church, close
at hand—for the notes of the horn phrase are virtually identical
with those of the last part of the 'Cambridge quarters.' " * The
audience believed that the apparent quotation was intentional on
Brahms's part, and so did I until refuted by his correspondence!
For years the First symphony was known in England as the
"Cambridge" symphony.

* "Brahms," by J. Fuller Maitland, London: Methuen & Co.,
Ltd., 1911.

precedes a chorale played softly by the trombones. Thereafter the horn-call, repeated, is answered by flute and trumpet, and this leads to the finale. Some have found in the theme that opens the last movement proper an imitation of Beethoven's theme in the finale of the Ninth symphony, and Brahms was pardonably irritated by the reminiscence hunters. The resemblance is one of only two measures and the analogy is far-fetched. The broad-arched theme chanted by the strings is the beginning of a movement that proceeds with a power and drama which are irresistible. A criticism of this victorious movement could be that it contained too many ideas and too rich development. But what could be omitted? It is a special test of a conductor's powers of synthesis.

●

Symphony No. 2, in D major, Opus 73

    I.   Allegro non troppo
   II.   Adagio non troppo
  III. Allegretto grazioso (quasi andantino)
  IV. Allegro con spirito

The lyrical beauty of Brahms's Second symphony makes it perhaps the most popular of the four works he composed in this form. The contrast between this symphony and the heroic First is complete, and it is strikingly analogous to the differences between Beethoven's Fifth and Sixth symphonies. Brahms's First and Beethoven's Fifth are both in the same key and in a heroic vein. Both composers took considerable time with these works, although Brahms, who was forty years old before his first symphony saw the light, was by far the more deliberate. Then, after the two C minor symphonies of storm and stress, each man produced, in a short time, a work which offered ingratiating contrast to previous epic utterances. Each of these works, furthermore, implies a "return to nature." Beethoven's symphony in F is avowedly so. The title "Pastoral," as well as the music, proves it. Brahms's D major symphony has no title; it is less impressionistic, closer knit and stronger in its fabric than the corresponding work of Beethoven; but it, too, is surely of nature, and its vernal loveliness is like unto that of the Spring.

The opening, with the four notes of the 'cellos and basses and the reply of the dusky horn, is the emotional as well as the musical key of the composition. The melodies that stream and intermingle in the orchestra, the lusty power of certain contrasting passages, and the coda, in which the magical horn is heard again, haunting forever the memory—all this is Spring herself, her dreaming eyes, her wayward glance. The second movement, grave and poetic, is Brahms in a brown study. For his contemporaries the movement was "a hard nut to crack." For us it is not so formidable. We know Brahms better, and admire him the more for his complete originality and fearlessness in self-expression. Here he thinks aloud. In his own way, and sometimes in long sentences, he formulates his thought, and the movement has the rich chromaticism, depth of shadow and significance of detail that characterize a Rembrandt portrait. It is also the admirable foil to the virility and élan of other movements. The third movement, with its delicious modulations and capricious changes of rhythms, is all built on the pastoral melody that the oboe sings over the strings pizzicato. The finale begins with a kind of theme that is a hallmark of Brahms's style— a motive played in unison by many instruments, which creeps mysteriously through the low registers of the orchestra before its brilliant proclamation by the full band. There are also rhythmical effects for which this composer has a fondness—alternating two and three rhythms, or groups of notes in these two rhythms, opposed to each other, and sudden explosive accents remindful of Beethoven. Later the violins take up a new song, having for its bass a motive from the opening theme of the movement, which later, flung out by the trumpets, brings the glorious conclusion. When Brahms had finished this symphony he wrote his friend, Dr. Billroth, saying, "I don't know whether I have a pretty symphony. I must inquire of learned persons!"

•

Symphony No. 3, in F major, Opus 90

    I.   Allegro con brio
   II.   Andante
 III.   Poco allegretto
 IV.   Allegro

Did Brahms ever write a more thrilling theme than the one which leaps from the orchestra like a bolt from Jove at the beginning of the Third symphony? And what is more poetical than the end of the symphony, when that same fury theme, or a fragment of it, is heard again in terms of sunset splendor? The symphony is a further development of Brahms's mastery of material, and variety of rhythms, and its nature is very romantic.

The first and last movements of the Third symphony are closely connected by theme and mood. These movements are heard, as it were, against a background of mountain, sky and singing winds. The two inner movements are in a different category. They are in fact less symphonic in character than the corresponding parts in any of the other Brahms symphonies. These inner parts of the Third symphony are smaller and more intimate in conception. Carefully as they are worked out, they have nevertheless such unity and mood that they sound almost as improvisations. Some feel that these movements are rather expansions of Brahms's chamber music style, or even of the structures of his shorter piano pieces, than appropriate for a great symphony. The more fanatical of

[173]

the "Brahmins," who are content with nothing but the most extravagant praises of "the master," will probably dispute this. For me the special effect of these movements lies precisely in their intimate and personal nature. They are cradled between the Jovian beginning and the towering finale as valleys lie between towering heights.

The second movement grows from a melody which has the character of a German folksong or lullaby. Its melodic offshoots cluster about the principal theme, with a brief passage of necessary contrast. The third movement is one of a compassionate melancholy and introspection, the principal theme given a special color by the combined tone of 'cello and clarinet. The "color" of this movement is not less original and unprecedented in orchestral music than the peculiar technic and poetical coloring, in another field, of Brahms's representative piano pieces. Schumann was not more personal. The finale is energetic and magnificent, and the last pages have the glory and serenity of the afterglow.

●

Symphony in E minor, No. 4, Opus 98

I. Allegro non troppo
II. Andante moderato
III. Allegro giocoso
IV. Allegro energico e passionato

It is very interesting to examine Brahms's progress as a symphonist. He appeared in the time of so-called

[174]

romanticism in music, when considerations of form were largely subordinated to subjective expression. Liszt was then creating his symphonic poems and Wagner his tremendous music-dramas—all works strongly colored by literary and poetic ideas, and by a very personal attitude on the part of the composer. Brahms, in his First symphony, if not an outright romanticist, is yet "romantic" in his attitude, just as Beethoven in his Fifth. Later on we are witness to Brahms's progression backward—or forward—from the "romantic" to the "classic" persuasion. The Fourth symphony is a pure classic masterpiece. From this, however, it is not to be assumed that the symphony is only a work of design, without subjective undercurrent. Quite the contrary! While Brahms has long since parted company with the storm and stress of the First symphony, the accents of the Fourth are in the highest degree charged with the resignation and the profound understanding that his own earnest nature and the passage of the years had brought him, and the nobility that existed under his crusty exterior. The romanticist has been purged of his passion. The fury and strife are gone. With them has gone the quality of action and drama which inspired earlier pages. But in the Fourth symphony something has replaced these things, something even more precious, and wiser.

It is perhaps significant that Brahms, ordinarily certain of himself and his work, had misgivings and questionings about this symphony. Did it touch more distant horizons than any to which he yet had raised his eyes? Or was he merely suffering from failing strength and ill-health? Or was he, as some might claim, affected by the spirit of a period which had seeds of decadence? Some find the symphony an expression of rank pessimism. They say that it is bitter, that it drips melancholy like the yew tree, that its thoughts are of death. But pessimism is not despair, nor need it be in any sense ignoble. If Brahms's thoughts at the time he wrote this symphony were turning toward his own end which was near, death must have appeared as it should appear to all of us, as a tender friend and a supreme consoler. It is a far cry from such a spirit and art as that of Brahms to the art of a Whitman. And yet there is something in this Fourth symphony which may well turn the memory to the words of the great American poet in "Out of the Cradle Gently Rocking," when he writes of the secret word that the waves kept whispering to the boy who watched the lonely nightbird from among the reeds on the shore. Here, in this symphony, are perhaps premonitions of the other side of life, vistas of a beauty linked with eternity, beauty as mysterious and inexplicable as the design of a pine tree against a flaming autumn sky.

The first movement begins with the lovely theme with which the orchestra is soon weaving arabesques. It continues with motives that supply the necessary

energy and masculinity to balance the more delicate
traceries; and all this is murmurous of some legendary
land, autumnal and infinitely beautiful. The second
movement is an exquisite play of ancient and modern
tonalities, hauntingly poetical and suggestive of distance. The motive of the solo horn is cast in the so-
called "Phrygian" mode (when the F-sharp and D-
sharp of E minor become F and D natural). Later on
this "modal" treatment gives place to a version of the
theme in the major key, with enchanting effect. But
in the third movement Brahms is again old bear's-
paws, with his feet on the good earth, rapping out his
rhythm in music that tingles with force, laughter and
joy.

The final movement is the great Passacaglia, capstone to the whole edifice. Some may find in it the
same esthetic significance as in the finale of Beethoven's "Eroica." On a theme eight measures long
are built masterly variations and a coda. The pervading motive is always present, in one or another form,
and with different orchestrations. It is variously altered and disguised, but if examined shows how closely
Brahms is sticking to his text. After each one of the
variants it would be fair to applaud, save that some
of them go too deep for applause and can only be
rendered silent homage. One of these is the twelfth
variation for the solo flute, over soft chords of horns
and violins; others are the fourteenth, with its chorale
for the trombones; the passionate seventeenth and

eighteenth; the song of the wind instruments in variation 28. But it is inadvisable and superfluous to confuse the listener by reference to details in this movement. Indeed, nothing is more striking than the manner in which the variations are put together. Thus the movement is not a series of episodes, but rather of linked evolutions of a single thought, with a final great sweep from the sixteenth variation, when the theme is uttered with such magnificent energy by the brass choir, to the end. It could be said that Brahms had been unconsciously preparing himself for the composition of this Passacaglia through many years of gradually acquired mastery of the variation form. The movement is his last symphonic will and testament. Some consider that the Fourth Symphony represents the end of a long musical epoch, and they explain its pervading spirit as the farewell of a master whose thoughts turned away from the present and back to the faith of his great forbears—Bach, Handel, Beethoven, Schubert. But this noble and reflective work appears more secure, and more rather than less in touch with living musical thought as the years pass. If this be resignation it is the resignation of strength, faith, awareness of the indestructibility of thought and beauty.

CAMILLE SAINT-SAËNS

1835–1921

Symphony No. 3, in C minor, Opus 78

I. Adagio; Allegro moderato; Poco adagio
II. Allegro moderato; Presto; Maestoso; Allegro

AND if you hunted through a hundred universes you could not find a man or artist so antithetical to Brahms of the Fourth symphony as Camille Saint-Saëns. We shall speak here only of his most notable symphony, and not of the four short and Gallic symphonic poems ("Le Rovet d'Omphale," "Phaëton," "La jeunesse d'Hercule," "La danse macabre") which had, at the time of their composition, a special importance in French music.

Saint-Saëns was, in the first place, a man of culture, of cosmopolitan experience, distinguished manners, travel and acquaintance with the great world. A brilliant musician and composer, a consummate technician and master of form, a true artist, he would nevertheless have wrought differently if he had possessed a greater soul. When Saint-Saëns visited this country in the season of 1906-1907, then a man of seventy-one years, to play with various orchestras and appear in other concerts of his own works, Philip Hale wrote of him in the Boston Symphony program

[179]

books of that season (and others), in part as follows:
"Organist, pianist, caricaturist, dabbler in science, enamored of mathematics and astronomy, amateur comedian, feuilletonist, critic, traveler, archæologist —he has been, and is, a restless man.

"He is of less than average height, thin, nervous, sick-faced; with great and exposed forehead, hair habitually short, beard frosted. His eyes are almost level with his face. His eagle-beak would have excited the admiration of Sir Charles Napier, who once exclaimed, 'Give me a man with plenty of nose.' Irritable, whimsical, ironical, paradoxical, indulging in sudden changes of opinion, he is faithful to friends, appreciative of certain rivals, kindly disposed towards young composers, zealous in practical assistance as well as in verbal encouragement. A man that knows the world and sparkles in conversation; fond of society; at ease and on equal terms with leaders in art, literature, fashion. A man whose Monday receptions were famous throughout Paris, eagerly attended by 'Tout Paris'; yet never so happy as when playing Calchas to Bizet's or Regnault's Helen in Offenbach's delightful 'La Belle Hélène' or impersonating in an extraordinary costume Gounod's Marguerite surprised by the jewels. . . . A Parisian from crown to sole; and yet a nomad. . . .

"In the face of difficulties, discouragement, misunderstanding, sneers, he has worked steadily since his youth and always to the best of his ability, for righteousness in absolute music; he endeavored to introduce into French music thoughtfulness and sincerity for the advantage and the glory of the country that he so dearly loves."

The highest praise should be Saint-Saëns's for his clear-headedness, conscience, and alertness in promoting the cause of symphonic music in France; for the fact that he fought prejudice and routine, and was consistently a pioneer of progress. When he composed his Third and most ambitious symphony, it was explained to the public that "the time has come for the symphony to benefit by the progress of modern instrumentation, and he [Saint-Saëns] therefore establishes his orchestra as follows: woodwind—three flutes, two oboes, one English horn, two clarinets, one bass clarinet, two bassoons, one double-bassoon; brass—four horns, three trumpets, three trombones, one tuba; three kettledrums; organ; piano (now for two hands, now for four); one triangle, a pair of cymbals, bass-drum, and the usual strings." An exposition, as Saint-Saëns designed it, of what the symphony formally and orchestrally had come to in his day.

This score is in fact a compendium of the things that had been done in symphonic composition up to that time (1886), particularly as regarded the transformation as well as the development of themes, and the attempt to give greater cohesiveness to the structure. The work is dedicated to Franz Liszt, between whom and Saint-Saëns there was much friendship and esteem, and Liszt's influence is clear in this symphony. In place of the traditional four movements, here are two, each part containing within itself two movements, joined together and roughly corresponding to those of the classic form. The first part projects a grave introduction, followed by a quicker section, which leads without a break into the equivalent of the slow movement of Haydn and Beethoven. The opening of the second part is freely in the manner of a scherzo, and it connects with the finale, ushered in by a majestic theme for trombone, tuba and double-basses. All the themes of the symphony have relation to each other. The theme heard after the introduction of the first part has a chance resemblance to the string accompaniment of the first theme of Schubert's "Unfinished" symphony. The principal melody of the slow movement, given the strings with organ accompaniment, is of ecclesiastical character. There is something of the sardonic in the energetic phrases which open the second part of the symphony. These phrases are in dramatic contrast to the majestic theme of the finale, already referred to, and these two themes might be considered as religious and demoniac elements contending for the mastery. Under such a definition the good triumphs; the evil is conquered and absorbed by it. The final passage, distinguished by orchestral pomp and flourish of trumpets, is a last transformation of the first theme of the symphony. Thus the symphony, which is Saint-Saëns's most pretentious work for orchestra, and too grand in its form for the actual strength of his ideas, is, on the other hand, anticipation of the so-called "cyclic" symphonies of César Franck and Vincent d'Indy and others of a later day of French music, of which Saint-Saëns is here revealed as one of the forerunners. The C minor symphony is testimony to his mastery, his seriousness, his clear realization of the significance of musical tendencies of his time. But it is a work symptomatic and not creative of a period.

PETER ILYITCH TCHAIKOVSKY

1840–1893

Symphony No. 4, in F minor, Opus 36

I.   Andante sostenuto; moderato con anima
      (in movimento di valse)
II.   Andantino in modo di canzona
III. Scherzo: Pizzicato ostinato; Allegro
IV. Finale: Allegro con fuoco

PETER ILYITCH TCHAIKOVSKY was a child
of the earth, and of the nation of Pushkin and Dostoievsky. Musical purists look down upon him. He
was not a classicist. He had not the heroic strength
and will of a Beethoven. He spoke in music as one
of the insulted and injured. He was all feeling. In his
scores he cries out, shakes his fist at the skies, remembers the agony of thwarted love, and the end of every
man's desire. Admire such a man, such a neurotic,
such a pessimist? I profoundly esteem and rate him a
thousand times higher than those who have never
known Tchaikovsky's weakness and terror, who shudder at such emotional indecencies, and pull their skirts
together at the sound of them. How can *they* know
what Tchaikovsky is saying?

George Moore remarked that we do not realize how
like our destiny is to ourselves. The first representative
symphony of Tchaikovsky—the three earlier ones are

negligible—would quite naturally treat of that monster Fate, against whom no man may prevail. Such a concept would be temperamental with this composer, and the undercurrent of much of his music. As it happened, the writing of this symphony was coincident with two events of momentous consequence to Tchaikovsky as man and composer. In these events two women were concerned. One secured him his creative career. The other almost terminated it.

In the early part of 1877 Tchaikovsky began the first movement of the Fourth symphony. In July he made a catastrophic marriage. A young woman had written a letter telling him that she loved him, and had pulled terribly on his heart-strings of pity. There was a scene—fit material for a Dostoievsky. In a mood, says the composer's brother, Modeste, of "abnormal and fatal exaltation" they agreed to marry. Tchaikovsky was in agony. "To live thirty years," he wrote a friend, "with an innate antipathy to marriage, and then suddenly, by force of circumstances, to find one's self engaged to a woman one does not love is very painful." It was all of that! The wretched man consoled himself "with the thought that we cannot escape our fate, and there was something fatalistic in my meeting with this girl." So he wrote to his guardian angel, Nadejda von Meck, the woman to whom he never spoke, but in letters poured out his soul. Soon after the wedding the composer made what may be termed an indirect attempt at suicide. Thirteen days after the housewarming he incontinently fled, with the appearance of a madman, and was two days unconscious. The doctors announced that it would be out of the question for Tchaikovsky and his wife ever to live together. But that was not all. What has not, up to the time of this writing, been published in any biography in English; what Tchaikovsky never told the world, or confided until years later to a friend, and what that friend, who was Kashkin, waited long to reveal, was the mental condition of the bride. She was subnormal, almost half-witted, which explains many of her later and otherwise incomprehensible actions, and eventually led to her being placed in an asylum! Undoubtedly ignorant of this when he married, Tchaikovsky never blamed his wife for what had taken place, and Modeste Tchaikovsky, whose biography of his brother is engrossing reading, contents himself with remarking that "following his [Tchaikovsky's] example, I cannot complete this chapter without exonerating her from all that happened." It was a pathological business all round!

It need hardly be said that during this time Tchaikovsky did not compose. The symphony lay unheeded, and would never have been finished had it not been for the woman whose noble and generous friendship makes a remarkable chapter in the history of music. Nadejda Filaretovna von Meck, the wealthy widow of a Russian engineer, had come to know Tchaikovsky through his music. She had given him commissions, and paid him so handsomely that the composer, though poverty-stricken, had finally refused to accept the sums, saying that he valued her friendship above her patronage. When, as a result of his marital *débâcle*, Tchaikovsky, penniless, had to be taken away from Russia and any reminder of former scenes, Madame von Meck provided the funds. At the same time she asked him to accept from her an annual pension which would free him from care and enable him to give his whole time to composition. To this gift, with infinite generosity and comprehension of his character—and with what wisdom!—she attached one condition, which was, that they should never meet. That gift was accepted in the spirit in which it was made, and the condition fulfilled. Tchaikovsky spent nearly two years outside Russia, living principally in Switzerland and Italy, gradually recovering from his shock. He carried his symphony with him in his wanderings, and by December, 1878, it was completed. His letters of that period to Madame von Meck are full of it—"our symphony," he calls it. The dedication is "To my best friend." This is the background of the Fourth symphony. Is it any wonder that the work is uneven and feverish, that the instrumentation is now brilliant and now black as night, that the figure of Fate, typified by a blaring fanfare of the brass, stalks imperious through the score?

There are four movements. The first is introduced

by the Fate theme. The music pursues a restless and fitful course. The motive of destiny twice intervenes. "So is all life," wrote Tchaikovsky to his patroness, "but a continual alternation between grim truth and fleeting dreams of happiness. There is no haven. The waves drive us hither and thither until the sea engulfs us. This is approximately the program of the first movement."

He says that "The second movement shows another phase of sadness. Here is that melancholy feeling which enwraps one when he sits alone in the house at night, exhausted by work; the book which he has taken to read slips from his hand; a swarm of reminiscences has risen. How sad it is that so much has already been and gone, and yet it is a pleasure to think of the early years. One mourns the past and has neither the courage nor the will to begin a new life. . . . And all that is now so far away, so far away."

Of the third movement Tchaikovsky wrote in an earlier letter that it would have "quite a new orchestral effect, from which I expect great things." It is the movement in which the three principal divisions of the orchestra—strings, woodwind and brass—are used in succession. This popular movement, the Scherzo, begins with the "pizzicato ostinato," in which the players pluck the strings instead of using the bow. The device has a fantastical effect, not unsuggestive of Autumn wind and whirling leaves. The wind instruments play a skirling tune. A march-like

passage for brass and kettledrums ensues. Finally fragments of all these three sections are tossed back and
forth by the instruments. "Here," wrote Tchaikovsky, "are capricious arabesques, vague figures which
slip into the imagination when one has taken wine
and is slightly intoxicated. The mood is now gay, now
mournful. One thinks about nothing; one gives the
fancy loose rein, and there is pleasure in drawings of
marvelous lines. Suddenly rushes into the imagination
the picture of a drunken peasant and a gutter-song.
Military music is heard passing in the distance. These
are disconnected pictures, which come and go in the
brain of the sleeper. They have nothing to do with
reality; they are unintelligible, bizarre, out at the el-
bows."

"Go to the people," he writes, in explanation of
his vodka-ridden finale. There is heard, soon after, a
crash of cymbals and whirling descent of strings, a
Russian folksong, "In the Fields There Stood a Birch-
tree," played by the woodwinds. This movement is
"the picture of a folk-holiday. Scarcely have you forgotten yourself, scarcely have you had time to be absorbed in the happiness of others, before untiring fate
again announces its approach. The other children of
men are not concerned with you. They neither see nor
feel that you are lonely or sad. . . . Rejoice in the
happiness of others—and you can still live." But the
rejoicing is hectic. It is interrupted again by the sar-

donic proclamation of Fate. The reckless conclusion is brilliant, yet akin to despair.

•

Symphony No. 5, in E minor, Opus 64

I.   Andante; Allegro con anima
II. Andante cantabile, con alcuna licenza
III. Valse: Allegro moderato
IV. Finale: Andante maestoso; Allegro vivace

Tchaikovsky's Fifth symphony has been variously rated. There is more disagreement as to its quality and value than about the Fourth or the Sixth. The composer himself was long dubious of its value. He wrote Madame von Meck in December of 1888, "After two performances of my new symphony I have come to the conclusion that it is a failure. There is something repellent, something superfluous, patchy, and insincere, which the public instinctively realizes. . . . The consciousness of this brings me a sharp twinge of self-dissatisfaction. . . . Last night I looked through *our* symphony [No. 4]. What a difference! How immeasurably superior it is! It is very, very sad!"

The Fifth symphony had come hard. For an interval its author had produced little. Now, with poor health and low spirits dogging him, he girded up his loins and set to work. In this place it is worth while to remark that despite his physical and temperamental difficulties, Tchaikovsky was a hard and systematic

[190]

workman. He did not wait for inspiration. He worked steadily, systematically at his task. This steadfastness, the more remarkable in one given to his despondencies, undoubtedly saved him in the creative field. If industry and system in working did not disperse his neuroticism, they counter-balanced it, and his capacity as a technician became the admirable servant of his inspiration. It may be said that when completed the Tchaikovsky Fifth symphony represented a conspicuous triumph, not only for the artist, but for the man.

For this music, singularly enough, has a certain relation to another Fifth—that of Beethoven, which hymns the universal drama of man pitted against fate. It is the only one of Tchaikovsky's symphonies which ends victoriously. Furthermore, both composers transform a thematic idea in accordance with an obviously dramatic conception. And here the resemblance ceases. For Beethoven salvation was a struggle, a vision and a faith. Only once was it given Tchaikovsky to entertain such confidence, and he never had Beethoven's classic structure or incisive power.

Like Tchaikovsky's Fourth symphony, his Fifth states the theme of destiny in the introduction, with clarinets and dark-hued instrumentation. The orchestra broods over this theme before entering upon the despondent or wildly dramatic moods of the first movement proper. A new motive stated by clarinet

[191]

and bassoons is dwelt upon at great length, as a thought that cannot be shaken off. Two other ideas appear in the course of the movement proper—one of them a mournful phrase in the rhythm of the waltz. But the persistent rhythm of the first theme dominates, and it echoes sadly from instrument to instrument in the concluding measures.

The second movement, introduced by sustained chords of the strings, is a scene of moonlight and romance, if ever there was one in symphonic music. The horn begins a ravishing song following preliminary harmonies of the strings. A second strain, given woodwind instruments, brings a more ardent mood. Then the strings, with a fine sweep, and elaborated orchestration, take up the song the horn first sounded. There is a sensuous climax, and new material as laden with lyrical feeling as the Spring night. After a second climax, the fate theme intervenes, grimly, sardonically, and the end is despondent.

The third movement is really a waltz, with a contrasting section in a different rhythm. It replaces the classic scherzo. It has a kind of a sick gayety. Toward the end the motto theme is woven into the dance like a specter that will not be laid.

But in the militant finale Tchaikovsky is another man. The theme of destiny is now heard as a triumphant proclamation in the major key, with panoply of the full orchestra. The trumpets are answered by salvos of the assembled instruments. A later theme is akin to Beethoven in its amplitude of line and its fine curve, set over a treading bass. Finally the whole orchestra prepares solemnly for the apotheosis, with the fate theme transfigured and glorified, and the composer captain of his soul.

•

Symphony No. 6 ("Pathetic"), in B minor, Opus 74

I. Adagio; Allegro non troppo
II. Allegro con grazia
III. Allegro molto vivace
IV. Finale: Adagio lamentoso

But there is no question: the "Symphonie Pathétique," Tchaikovsky's Sixth and last, is his masterpiece, one which will endure as long as any of his music is known. Nowhere else has he approached the burning intensity and the sable splendor of this score. In no other place has he revealed himself with equal completeness and mastery of expression. The "Symphonie Pathétique" made such an impression upon the public that for a time it was overplayed. Thereafter it was underpraised. It remains a human document of immense pathos and tragedy. Some are repelled by the hysteria and self-laceration of pages of the music. To this it can only be replied that each of us has a right to the music we like, and vice versa; and that so far as Tchaikovsky was concerned, he never could compose from a safe place. He had a profound humanity

[193]

and a native sweetness and tenderness, with a tortured sensibility. And he was a very gifted composer. Suffering and knowledge overwhelmed him. The eyes of his spirit saw things they would fain not have seen. He tells us what they saw in a voice that often chokes with rage and pity.

This symphony was Tchaikovsky's swan song. Nine days after its first performance, which he conducted, he died of cholera, and the circumstances of his taking off were so sudden as to give rise to the theory, still widely believed, that following his tonal deposition he committed suicide. There is, however, no reason to doubt Modeste Tchaikovsky's account of his brother's end, told in one of the most fascinating of musical biographies. Tchaikovsky drank a glass of unboiled water and contracted the disease that sent him quickly to his grave. Some curious coincidences gave added color to the suicide theory, such as the fact that the composer had busied himself in the months preceding with the clearing up of documents, revisions of scores, and the destruction of personal records. These, however, appear only as the actions of a methodical worker. Existence had been cruel enough to furnish Tchaikovsky with more than material for a tragic symphony. His essentially noble and compassionate nature, his strange and frustrated relations with life, were sufficient to darken any spirit. The man's inordinate craving for affection had been cruelly wounded by the estrangement of Mathilde von Meck, whose name Tchaikovsky uttered reproachfully in his dying delirium. He did not know that his former bene-factress and dearest friend had become the victim of mental derangement, nor was he the man to believe that on the other side of the grave the needful word of understanding could be uttered.

Nevertheless, Tchaikovsky was happy in the cre-ation of this symphony. He knew that he had achieved *his* truth, and produced a great work, despite its cold reception at the first performance. Some historians, Modeste among them, say that the coldness of the audience was due to the fact that Tchaikovsky con-ducted. He was not an effective leader or interpreter even of his own music. He could not face an orches-tra with confidence, still less force it to do his exact bidding. A musician who played under him has told us of a rehearsal with the composer on the conductor's stand—frightened, apologetic, and ever and anon fur-tively reaching to his back pocket for a flask of cour-age. But Rimsky-Korsakoff heard the first perform-ance of the "Pathétique"; he says that the only fault was the public's slowness to appreciate such an original score. Be all that as it may, Tchaikovsky was well aware that his Sixth symphony was "the best, especi-ally the *most open-hearted* [ours the italics] of all my works." To his colleague Ippolitoff-Ivanoff, a kindly old man who lives and flourishes in Moscow at the time of this writing, he wrote, "I told you I had completed a symphony which suddenly displeased me, and I tore it up. Now I have composed a symphony *which I certainly shall not tear up*." He sends a similar message to Jurgenson, the publisher: "I give you my word that never in my life have I been so contented, so proud, so happy, in the knowledge that I have written a good piece." It is hard to dismiss regretful thoughts of what Tchaikovsky might have accomplished, now that he had fully discovered himself as an artist, if he had lived beyond fifty-three.

Tchaikovsky let it be known that this symphony had a story, but he did not tell what that story was, which is fortunate, since the work is so much greater than any plot could be. But there was the question of naming the symphony—which, by the way, he had sketched on the ocean during his return to Russia from America in 1891. The morning after the first performance of the work from manuscript in what was then St. Petersburg, October 28, 1893, Modeste Tchaikovsky found his brother at a tea-table with the music in his hand. The composer wanted to bestow some title more definite than that of "Symphony No. 6" before sending the score to the publisher. What should it be? Should it be, for example, "Program Symphony"? But what did that signify if the symphony was given no program? Modeste suggested "Tragic," but Tchaikovsky was not satisfied. Modeste left the room; when on the other side of the door the word "Pathetic" came to him, and he returned. Tchaikovsky was delighted. "Splendid,

Modi, bravo! 'Pathetic' "—"And he wrote in my presence," says Modeste, "the title that will always remain."

The symphony has an unusual succession of movements and peculiarities of form. The last movement,
for example, is not a brilliant ending, but a dirge.
The most exciting movement is the one before the last
—the terrible march. There is no slow movement, but
instead, for the second part, a dance in the strange
and perturbing rhythm of five-four. It will be seen
that the symphonic structure is here wholly subor-
dinate to the subjective idea.

The first movement exposes immediately a principal theme, clad in the blackest colors of the orchestra.
Yes! it is pitch-black, and brother to the worm. With
the quick tempo of the major part of the movement,
fragments of this theme are tossed from instrument
to instrument. Now it is picked to pieces by wind or
strings; now it is shrieked hysterically by the trumpet.
In spite of the length and diversity of the movement,
with its many dramatic episodes, the composer paints
his picture with extraordinary concentration and with
passionate distinctness. He obtains from his instruments extraordinary effects of blackness contrasted
with flaring light, as when, early in the movement,
the despairing cry of the trumpet cuts through the
whizzing strings; or when, over yawning depths, the
trombones sound a spectral chant, taken, according
to Edwin Evans, from the Russian Requiem. At one

moment the orchestra sings passionately. At another
it lashes itself to frantic pitches of excitement, or
falls to yet deeper levels of lassitude. It is a striking
fact that the main theme, so prevalent throughout
the movement, never returns in its complete original
form. It is the haunting second theme which retains
its exact shape and most appealing melodic curve.
That theme is as strongly distinguished by its instrumentation as by its melody. It is given the violins
with an effect of torturing and undismissable re-
membrance. It is thrown into the greater prominence,
on repetition, by the richness of its orchestral dress.

A climax, very originally conceived, precedes the
return of this second theme. It follows an eruption of
tone, after which the orchestra hurtles downward to
depths which shudder and roar with rage—a passage
made from the introductory theme. This detail of
structure is cited as further testimony to the manner
in which a composer of genius makes form and feeling one. The movement, for Tchaikovsky, is one of
unprecedented richness of ideas, development and orchestration. Compared with this writing in this symphony, the best pages of preceding works are thin.
And note the pizzicato scale which persistently descends, like inexorable destiny, as epilogue of the first
movement.

The second movement is in the famous "five-four"
rhythm, and a rare example of the rhythmic problem
of five beats solved with entire naturalness. If the

LISTENER

reader will reflect and experiment a little with the
music he knows, he will quickly perceive that most
melodies fall into patterns of either two beats or
three beats or their multiples. The five-beat pattern
is not symmetrical. It is instinctive, ordinarily, to
make the five a design of either four or six. The conventional number of beats would here be six. But the
music flows with astonishing naturalness, while the
restlessness of the essentially asymmetrical arrangement is psychologically the truth of his unrest. It is
in the alternative section of this five-four movement
that Tchaikovsky makes unforgettable use of the
drum. The drum relentlessly pounds the measure, its
note rising and falling, while the strings wail over the
dull thudding beat. Card

This is original, but the third movement is more astounding. Its desperate festivity is false, brutal and
sardonic. Its psychological explanation is perhaps that
of a neurotic and hysterical nature which keys itself
up, for the moment, to a pitch of unconditional defiance and unnatural power. The wild and fantastic
music passes like a nightmare. The beginning, with
its whirling tonal will o' the wisps and evil exhilaration
as of something unholy a-brewing, could accompany
the scene of the witches on the heath in "Macbeth."
And now the solo oboe snarls a first intimation of
the march. From over the other side of the world a
trombone and then a horn reply, and one remembers
De Quincey's opium dream in which he heard music

of preparation and suspense, and the sound of cavalcades filing off in the distance to the battlefield where
an issue of undecipherable vastness was to be decided
—an issue involving all human fate. There is indeed
dreadful portent in this march of Tchaikovsky's, for
which Mr. Hale, whom it is difficult not to quote,
coined the one word—"battle-drunk."

In spite of all the stirrings and anticipations, it is
some time before the entire march theme is heard.
The composer holds back his forces with an astonishing grip and control in preparation. There is here no
going off half-loaded, as in other of Tchaikovsky's
works. He stares you in the eye, an unswerving stare.
The music gathers at his imperious command. The
hordes of Russia and the battalions of mankind file
by. Their tread shakes the earth, while the trumpets
scream salute, and banners are flung to the sky. Hail
Cæsar! The unearthly cavalcade draws nearer. The
march theme, heard first in fragments, has bit by bit
pulled itself out like a lengthening telescope. The
movement is a quarter completed when the clarinets,
with various orchestral rejoinders, round out the
theme. And the fury of the march accumulates. It
sees red it chokes with choler. Drums and brass instruments go into an incoherent fury. Perhaps you
did not know that a scale could become delirium?
Listen to the sizzling scales of the string and wind
sections that answer each other in Tchaikovsky's orchestra. At the last, quite suddenly, this orchestra sub-

sides; it crouches like a beast, and then advances; it boils up over everything; it crashes down to destruction. *"card"*

And this is the prelude to the inevitable end. In the finale the strings make requiem. Repeating the opening phrase, they sweep upward in a great sigh for poor vanquished life and the eternal farewell to warm and beautiful things. Over a pulsation of the horns a new threnody is sung. The orchestra rises and falls over a vibrating organ point, following which muted horns evilly mutter, and the gong tolls, and trombones intone a solemn chant. Then the melody that the horns accompanied is given the strings, which mournfully discourse together, until the phrase gradually disappears in the shadows. But a note of the double-basses persists a long time, like a throbbing pulse that will not be still.

This symphony is the last utterance of a great artist and an unfortunate man.

after music

ANTONIN DVOŘÁK

1841–1904

Symphony No. 5, in E minor ("From the New World"), Opus 95

    I.   Adagio; Allegro molto
    II.   Largo
    III. Scherzo: Molto vivace
    IV. Finale: Allegro con fuoco

THE famous "New World" symphony was one of the creative results of Dvořák's visit to America, where he taught composition at the National Conservatory of Music, 1892 to 1895. As a peasant with little education but extraordinary musical impressionability and creative power, and one profoundly attached to his own soil, Dvořák utilized Czech melodies in his scores, and his own melodic ideas were in the vein of Czech folk-music. Thus he became the principal exponent of the Czech national school of composition, just as Grieg in Norway headed a national school, and as a whole group of brilliant Russians, from Glinka to Rimsky-Korsakoff and Mussorgsky, founded their native school, which derived its inspiration largely from Russian folk-melody. Much might be said here about the folk-element in art music. Many believe that unless the roots of a composer's art are deep in the soil of his folk-melody, he cannot be significantly creative.

But we are now discussing Dvořák. Dvořák's instinct as a composer caused him to examine American folksongs, especially those of the negroes and Indians, with a view to incorporating their melodic essence, or spirit, in an American symphony. The appearance of the "New World" symphony, which is a charming and highly original score, precipitated long and academic discussion. The discussion is principally a thing of the past. The symphony remains. Whether it deserves the title of "New World" symphony, whether Dvořák did or did not use melodic ideas peculiar to America (though not folk-music of the present white Americans), is no longer of first importance. Dvořák himself denied that he had used Negro or American folk-tunes in his score, but there is one theme which is unmistakably derived from the Negro spiritual "Swing low, sweet chariot." It is given to a solo flute, against a background of strings, in the first movement. While the quotation is not precise, some notes of the original phrase being omitted, the source and the close resemblance are unquestionable. Harry T. Burleigh, the Negro choir singer of St. George's Church in New York, was a student at the National Conservatory of Music when Dvořák was teaching there, and he sang for the composer many Negro spirituals. "Swing low" was one of Dvořák's favorites. Most of the melodies in the symphony appear to be

Dvořák's, though the song of the English horn in the slow movement can well have originated in a Negro spiritual. It is in that vein, and it has a typical melancholy and pathos. As for the general character of the music, its pervading sentiment, or, as it might be put, temperament, it is after all that of a simple Czech, homesick for his native land. Yet the symphony comes fairly by the title "New World," not merely because of Dvořák's purpose in writing it, and the influence of music he found here, but because of the precipitating effect that the New World had upon his creative nature. "A greeting to the New World" might better have been a more precise indication of the nature of the composition. Certain it is that the feelings which stirred Dvořák's heart when he was here, and the effect of the new environment, inspired what is by far his greatest work in the symphonic form.

The symphony is in four movements, each with a few introductory measures. Themes are carried over, and thus accumulate, as the composer progresses. In the broad introduction the French horns anticipate a motive to be heard later. This motive, which appears in its complete form when the pace has quickened, is a basic element of the whole symphony. Another motive, which spans the space between this first theme and that of "Swing low, sweet chariot," is played first by flutes and oboes, and was believed by Mr. Burleigh to be derived from slave songs.[1] Following this the

[1] His letter, published in the Boston Symphony Program Book

solo flute is heard with the fragment of "Swing low, sweet chariot," which is then taken up by the strings. Thereafter all the material is developed according to symphonic usage. The noble harmonies of wood and brass which open the second movement prelude the song of the English horn already referred to. It is said that in this movement Dvořák had thought of certain parts of Longfellow's poem "Hiawatha," a subject which he considered making into an opera. The middle part of the movement is more animated, and it is not hard to think of a summer night on the prairie. Dvořák's scherzo, very piquant and brilliant, with a delightful melody in the manner of a peasant dance for its middle section, is decidedly Slavic. The opening theme of the last movement, crashed out by trumpets, with chords of the full orchestra, has a finely stark and barbaric outline. Is this an Indian influence? History does not tell us. This finale has a broad sweep and splendor, a fine glow of romantic feeling—a salutation to the New World.

Whether Americans could ever follow successfully in Dvořák's footsteps and create an important art from the folk-music of other peoples than themselves is a question still to be answered in the affirmative.

---

of December 20 and 21, 1930, and other program books of that organization, said that "There is a subsidiary theme in G minor in the first movement with a flatted seventh, and I feel sure the Doctor [Dvořák] caught this peculiarity of most of the slave songs from some that I sang to him; for he used to stop me and ask me if that was the way the slaves sang."

When Dvořák composed the "New World" symphony the American Edward MacDowell was already
at work upon his "Indian Suite." Years after Dvořák
and MacDowell too had disappeared, MacDowell's
most gifted American pupil, Henry F. Gilbert, produced certain scores which were pronounced by
Philip Hale, H. T. Parker and others to have authentic and distinctive American flavor. These scores utilized Negro spirituals and other folk-music. And now,
after a Gilbert did the spade-work and died, it is posi-
tively fashionable to write in jazz style. But the course
that American music will take in the future is not
easily predictable.

Dvořák, the starving son of a village butcher, had
taken his viola under his arm, played at fairs, country
weddings, and the like, wandered the highways and
byways of Bohemia, harkened to the music of the
gypsies and poured the accumulation, plus his own immense melodic fertility, into his scores. Why, he
asked, could not Americans do the same? For many
reasons. We have not developed a deep consciousness
of our soil. Our transplantation here is recent. We
cannot tell Europeans, as Will Rogers did, that while
his people did not come over on the *Mayflower*, they
met the boat! We have not, unfortunately, Dvořák's
feeling for nature. The machine age has come upon
us. Oscar Thompson, when he was music reviewer for
the New York "Evening Post," asked in the course of
a certain article what had become of the great Ameri-

can music we all expected to hear—music which should proclaim the beauty and romance of the new vast land, the sweep of mountain and prairie, the mystery of virgin forests, the glory of the stars. He answered himself. He said that the stars twinkled from electric fixtures in the roofs of road-houses and cabarets, and not from the night skies that overhang mountain and prairie. For we have gone urban and not rural in our development, and away from Dvořák's vision, not toward it. We have run to factories and hotels. Our most indigenous music is jazz, a town product. Even the simple lays of Negro minstrelsy are things of the past.

NICHOLAS RIMSKY-KORSAKOFF

1844–1908

Symphonic Suite, "Scheherazade" (after "The Thousand Nights and a Night"), Opus 35

I. The Sea and Sindbad's Ship
II. The Story of the Kalandar-Prince
III. The Young Prince and the Young Princess
IV. Festival at Baghdad. The Sea. The Ship goes to pieces on a Rock surmounted by a Bronze Warrior. Conclusion.

EVERYTHING conspired to make of Rimsky-Korsakoff a magician of the orchestra and an unsurpassed spinner of musical yarns. As a composer he belonged to the famous group whose purpose it was to base their works upon Russian folklore, folk-melody and popular artistic expression characteristic of their native land. In this material of folk-music and legend, the Oriental element, while not all-pervading, was very potent, so that Jean Marnold remarked that over Rimsky-Korsakoff Oriental monody seemed to cast a spell. While this does not hold true of all Rimsky-Korsakoff's music, it is extremely characteristic of such works as the "Antar" symphony and the "Scheherazade" symphonic suite.

As a musician, in his transformation of themes and wizardry of orchestral color, Rimsky-Korsakoff

[208]

was especially indebted to Berlioz and Liszt—not to Wagner and not to any of the symphonists of the German school. With his associates, Balakireff, Borodin, Cui and Mussorgsky, Rimsky-Korsakoff believed that the German symphonic method was not characteristic of the Russian spirit of which he sought in his music to be a true representative. The objectives of this famous group variously known as "the Cabinet," "The Five," or, in their own gallant phraseology, "The Invincible Band," were achieved in music unmistakably Russian in idiom and color and fantasy. Perhaps a phase of personal experience also contributed indirectly to the character of pages of the "Scheherazade" music. This was Rimsky-Korsakoff's experience of the sea. For he was a naval officer in his youth, having worked his way up from the rank of midshipman. He knew the oceans. He even visited the United States in 1862, and during that voyage sketched his first and rather inconsequential symphony. It should be added, however, that the sea Rimsky-Korsakoff portrays is neither that of Sandy Hook nor of Boston Harbor. It is an affair of the Bosporous and the Golden Horn. Its waters are inhabited by monsters and sirens. They are subject to strange spells. A ship may here find itself being transported on the back of a whale or it may be smashed into a thousand fragments by colliding with the Rock surmounted by the Bronze Warrior. In short, this is the sea which laved the shores where *Scheherazade*

lived and where she saved her neck for a thousand and
one nights by her incredible tales.

I had the right preparation for hearing the music
of "Scheherazade" when it was more novel in America
than it is today. There was first the rich and fantastical cover design of the piano duet arrangement of
which a copy, by chance, had crossed the seas and
landed in my lap. This design with its mosaics was
delightfully evocative of mosque and minaret, cres-
cents and scimitars, and the deep hard colors of the
old ikons. And then I knew the opening lines of Pushkin's prologue to "Russlan and Ludmilla"—Pushkin,
the well-spring, as one may say, not only of Russia's
poetry but of that national essence which was to per-
meate a national art school of composition and find its
way into Rimsky-Korsakoff's music. Those lines, as
translated by Madame N. Jarintzova, run like this:

> Near the sea-cove an oak is growing;
> Around that oak a golden chain:
> Along that chain Sir Cat-the-knowing
> Doth ever walk and walk again.
> Goes to the right—a song he chanteth,
> Goes to the left—a tale he tells.
> 'Tis wonderland: there wood fiend haunteth,
> And Mermaid 'mid the branches dwells.
> There are strange paths, the spoor betraying
> Of beasts that to no eye appear;
> A hut on chickens' legs, displaying
> No windows and no doors, is here.
> The dale and forest teem with vision.
> At early dawn, with neat precision,

The waves upon the beach unfold,
And thirty warriors young and splendid
File from the lucid deep, attended
By their sea-guardian grave and old. . . .

. . . .

There I have been; there I drank mead,
Saw the green oak near sea-cove growing,
And sat beneath; Sir Cat-the-knowing
Did with his wondrous tales proceed.

The four movements of "Scheherazade," the symphonic suite after "The Thousand Nights and a Night," are bound together by two representative themes, repeated and variously transformed as by a wave of the magician's wand in the course of the composition. First is the formidable pronouncement of the trombones, the magician's formula, the word of command. To this motive wind instruments respond with worshipful harmonies. And now the solo violin—the voice of *Scheherazade*, wheedling, beguiling, fantastically preluding her tale. The first one is the story of a voyage of "Sindbad the Sailor." This, at least, is the caption that the composer put over the music. We need not take it too seriously. We may imagine much what we please. The imaginative character of the headings placed over passages of the score shows that Rimsky-Korsakoff's purpose was rather to suggest the color and atmosphere of his fantasy than to bind us literally to any specific incident. But in this music it is easy to conceive the sound and the sight of the sea: the rocking of the boat on the waters; the scream

[211]

of wind in the rigging; even, if you like, the splash
of a wave against the hull. Or am I too willing to
believe the old enchanter? By a few passes of his wand,
by the transformation under your very nose of the
trombone motive of the introduction he evolves, by
hocus pocus, what you may believe to be the picture
of the tossing waters. And this motive, this sorcerer's
device, works its marvels through the whole score. It
companions the adventure of the Kalandar-Prince; it
vibrates amid the din and commotion of the bazaars
of the fair; it becomes at last the triumphant chant and
eternal menace of the sea which sent Prince Ajib's ship
to destruction.

What happens to the Kalandar-Prince on his adventures may not be specifically known to us. There
is more than one "Kalandar" in the Arabian Nights.
Sometimes it is a porter; sometimes a prince in dis-
guise. The translation of the tales by Sir Richard Bur-
ton will tell you more about them than I dare. This
particular tale of the orchestra begins with the rakish
narrative of the solo bassoon—a phrase you might hear
mongered by a merchant squatting in his bazaar; a
ditty that might have fallen on the ears of *Haroun-al-
Raschid* when he wandered disguised through the
streets of Baghdad. But this is only the beginning of
the queer yarn. Trumpet-calls sound from near by
and are answered from afar. Cavalcades file off to
war. In the desert anything can happen. There are
subdued petitions of terrified suppliants in the chords

of the plucked strings, and responses from wind instruments that wail strangely. Or, perchance, a service
in the mosque?

"The Prince and the Princess." Again—which ones?
This is an Oriental love song, set forth by an orchestra which simply splashes color, decorated with
sweeps of the harps and unbelievable clarinets and
flutes which fly up and down the scale, and fantastic
figures of the strings—drawing, as it were, the long
bow!

And now, in the final movement, hear the odd
rhythms, the thrummings, the cries, the shrillings of
wind-instruments at an Oriental festival—an intoxicating and previously unimagined series of effects.
Feel the dizzy acceleration of the ship doomed to
destruction, and the crash of the impact; and now the
sea music of the first movement, roared out by the
trombones, with clashing cymbals and waves of orchestral tone which mount over the hymning brass
as a great wave mounts and breaks over the swimmer's
head. . . . At last the ocean has calmed. The sea motive heaves deep in the basses of the orchestra, while
above the jeweled orchestration gives us colors like
those of a sunset sky. Once more *Scheherazade*
triumphs as the solo violin ascends in the orchestra,
and the wind instruments repeat the worshipful harmonies of the introduction—Salaam Aleikum!—
Homage to Rimsky, the old sorcerer, and his power.

[213]

VINCENT D'INDY

1851–1931

"Istar," Symphonic Variations, Opus 42

Towards the immutable land, Istar, daughter of Sin, bent her steps, towards the abode of the dead, towards the seven-gated abode where He entered, towards the abode whence there is no return.

At the first gate, the warder stripped her; he took the high tiara from her head.

At the second gate, the warder stripped her; he took the pendants from her ears.

At the third gate; the warder stripped her; he took off the precious stones that adorn her neck.

At the fourth gate, the warder stripped her; he took off the jewels that adorn her breast.

At the fifth gate, the warder stripped her; he took off the girdle that encompasses her waist.

At the sixth gate, the warder stripped her; he took the rings from her feet, the rings from her hands.

At the seventh gate, the warder stripped her; he took off the last veil that covers her body.

THESE lines, translated by William Foster Apthorp from a French version of the Babylonian poem of *Istar's* descent into Hades, are printed in d'Indy's score as preface to a remarkable series of variations.

Istar was goddess of fertility, hence sexual love, and

also of love's antithesis, war. When she descended to rescue her lover from the kingdom of Allatus, the Land of No Return, the earth ceased to create life. *Istar* was hated by the *Queen of the Shades,* who invoked disease and destruction upon her. But *Istar* found her lover. According to the last lines of the French translation of the poem, she "went into the immutable land, she took and received the Waters of Life. She gave the sublime Waters, and thus, in the presence of all, delivered the Son of Life, her young lover." The fierce *Queen Allatu* was placated. She permitted *Istar* to return to the upper world. Her garments—were they not those of Spring?—were returned to her at each of the seven gates, and again the earth was fertile and beautiful.

But we need not concern ourselves here with interpretation of the Assyrian allegory. The unique characteristic of d'Indy's score is its reversal of the composer's customary procedure with a theme and variations, a reversal of order dictated by the lines of the poem. For this is not a theme and variations. It is a set of variations and theme. The most ornate variations come first and the theme, in its complete and glowing simplicity does not emerge until the last, when it is sung resplendently by the orchestra with the thought of *Istar* in her naked splendor.

The Orientalism of d'Indy is far from that of Rimsky-Korsakoff, yet there is in his introduction a certain languorousness which might well be associated with the East. First, the orchestra broods over fragments of the theme; then, like the spread of a peacock's wing, the theme bursts forth, laden with trills and all sorts of instrumental decorations. One of its metamorphoses in the following pages is a variation in an irregular rhythm of seven beats, with rapid glinting effects in the high registers of wind instruments. It has been said that the composer meant to hint of the glittering jewels of which the goddess is deprived. The variations are cunningly juxtaposed. The one just before the last is boldly outlined by the instruments playing in unison without any supporting harmony or variety of tone color. This throws into higher relief the final apotheosis of the theme, sung in octaves by the strings of the orchestra, with a counterpoint for the solo horn marching underneath. Each variation is a remarkable manifestation of the power of d'Indy's musical mind and of the special type of his imagination.

D'Indy, a wholly individual figure in the history of French music, and one who stood apart from the somewhat decadent spirit of his times, had a passion for a beauty beyond the merely sensuous. He was an opponent of impressionism, and foe to that which was super-refined or defeatist in the modern French musical art.

ENGELBERT HUMPERDINCK

1854–1921

Overture to "Hänsel und Gretel"

THE overture to the opera "Hänsel und Gretel" is one of the most charming pages of post-Wagnerian music. The text of the opera, based upon the Grimm fairy tale, was written by Humperdinck's sister, Frau Adelheid Wette, for her children. Humperdinck had more than once composed music for such entertainments. He was much intrigued by the story of the two children lost in the wood and captured by a witch, whom they outwit by learning her spell, thus saving themselves and other children she had turned into gingerbread.

In due course the composer suggested that this subject be arranged in operatic form, and promised to write the score. The conductor Hermann Levi learned of the project. Later he obtained Humperdinck's permission to perform at a Munich concert the "Dream Pantomime"—the music for the scene in which the children fall asleep in the dark wood and are visited in their dreams by angels who descend a Jacob's Ladder and surround them. From that moment the fate of the opera was sealed. Levi wished to produce it, but a young man named Richard Strauss got ahead of him. Strauss, twenty-nine years of age, was then second conductor at the Weimar Court Theater. He asked permission to examine the score, and the enthusiasm of the composer of vast and problematic tone-poems for this delightful and innocent creation was unbounded. He wrote Humperdinck, in words that hold as true now as they did then: "It is a masterwork of the first rank. . . . What fresh humor, what charming, naïve melody, what art and delicacy in the handling of the orchestra, what fine invention, what splendid polyphony—and all original, new and so genuinely German! My dear friend, you are a great master, who has given to our people a work which they scarcely deserve, although it is to be hoped that they will soon value it at its true importance."

Humperdinck's fairy opera produced at Weimar—December 23, 1893. It quickly spread through Germany to the rest of Europe and to America. It is Humperdinck's one important work, the only music from his pen that will outlive him. There are such men—composers of one opera who concentrate in a single score all their genius. Humperdinck was reproached, and with some justice, for his employment of the immense Wagnerian orchestra for the music of a child's fairy tale. This was instinctive with him. He was a Wagner disciple. He had helped Wagner prepare

the "Parsifal" performances of 1880 and 1881 at
Bayreuth. He was the teacher in composition of Wagner's son, the late Siegfried. The immense, luminous,
polyphonic Wagnerian orchestra was his natural instrumental speech. He did not plagiarize Wagner's
music, but employed his orchestra. When Humperdinck dressed his themes in elaborate counterpoint
he was not only following Wagnerian method but
that substantial manner of composition which is the
expression of the German nature. It is true that the
orchestration of "Hänsel und Gretel" is weighty, that
a barrelful of notes taken out of the score at certain
places would only clarify it. But this proportion of
sediment, as Huneker remarked of Brahms, is naturally a part of the brew. It does not contaminate the
flavor. The overture begins and ends with the prayer
sung by the children before they fall asleep in the
wood. The quick movement is ushered in by the solo
trumpet with the music of the witch's spell, heard in
the opera to the words, "Hocus, pocus, elderbush."
Other themes of the fairy play are woven into the
fabric of the melodious, apple-cheeked music.

CLAUDE ACHILLE DEBUSSY

1862–1918

Prelude to "The Afternoon of a Faun"

(After the Eclogue by Stéphane Mallarmé)

DEBUSSY'S vaporous and iridescent score, which is like unto a dream within a dream, and of which no sonority rises above a moderate forte, is nevertheless a revolutionary document; and the beauty of the revolution is its noiselessness. This is really the first effective revolt against Wagnerism and Germanism in the orchestral music of the late nineteenth century, and it is conclusive. The old régime is out and the new one is in, without a cannon fired! No guns! No soap-box oratory! Debussy goes quietly away from the fuss and turmoil into his tower of ivory. He consults his own spirit and that of his antique culture and civilization. His music, in fact, goes back to a period before Bach and Beethoven ever existed, for it is essentially pagan, non-ethical, unphilosophic, and worshipful of beauty as it was known to the wise of an ancient world. Its workmanship is equally precise and subtle, and it has, in its finest manifestations, the indestructibility of the perfect thought. But Debussy does not pursue the methodical and symmetric

[220]

CLAUDE DEBUSSY

ideal of the German symphonists. He develops a
theme—yes—and squeezes the juice out of it as surely
as ever Beethoven did; but in place of an ordained
procedure, a scheme of architecture, determined in
advance, Debussy seems to set his themes free, to let
them wing their way untrammeled through space, or
float indolently on the current of his deep-tinted harmonies, as if the melody followed a will of its own
which had nothing at all to do with the clumsy arti-
fices of man.

Debussy associated intimately with painters, poets
and writers of his period. He was sympathetic with
the impressionistic painters, and with that outgrowth
of impressionism, the "symbolist" school of poetry, of
which the leader was Stéphane Mallarmé. The sym-
bolists sought not only an approach to musical effect
by means of rhythm, assonance and rhyme; they
sought also something deeper—the evocation, by
means of the sounds and of words, of subconscious
sensations and ideas. Hence the text of Mallarmé's
eclogue, "L'Après-midi d'un Faune," is intentionally
vague, obscure of meaning, as elusive in its images as
Debussy's music. Edmund Gosse's elucidation is generally accepted as a trustworthy interpretation of the
poem. This poem, after being rejected by the "Par-
nasse Contemporain," in 1875, was published in 1876,
with illustrations by the painter Manet. Gosse, who
spoke of Mallarmé's use of words in a manner to "suggest to the reader a mood or a condition which is *not*

mentioned in the text" (the italics are mine), remarked of the verse:

"To say that I understand it bit by bit, phrase by phrase,
would be excessive. But, if I am asked whether this famous
miracle of unintelligibility gives me pleasure, I answer,
cordially, Yes. I even fancy that I obtain from it as definite
and as solid an impression as M. Mallarmé desires to produce. This is what I read in it: A faun—a simple, sensuous,
passionate being—wakens in the forest at daybreak and
tries to recall his experience of the previous afternoon. Was
he the fortunate recipient of an actual visit from nymphs,
white and golden goddesses, divinely tender and indulgent?
Or is the memory he seems to retain nothing but the
shadow of a vision, no more substantial than the 'arid rain'
of notes from his own flute? He cannot tell. Yet surely
there was, surely there is, an animal whiteness among the
brown reeds of the lake that shines out yonder? Were they,
are they, swans? No! But Naiads plunging? Perhaps!
Vaguer and vaguer grows the impression of this delicious
experience. He would resign his woodland godship to retain it. A garden of lilies, golden-headed, white-stalked,
behind the trellis of red roses? Ah! the effort is too great
for his poor brain. Perhaps if he selects one lily from the
garth of lilies, one benign and beneficent yielder of her cup
to thirsty lips, the memory, the ever-receding memory,
may be forced back. So when he has glutted upon a bunch
of grapes, he is wont to toss the empty skins into the air
and blow them out in a visionary greediness. But no, the
delicious hour grows vaguer; experience or dream, he will
never know which it was. The sun is warm, the grasses
yielding; and he curls himself up again, after worshipping
the efficacious star of wine, that he may pursue the dubious
ecstasy into the more hopeful boskages of sleep."

[222]

I remember well when Debussy's score was first heard in America. It produced an impression of subtlety and evanescence that the ear might not grasp, to say nothing of the mind. "L'Après-midi d'un Faune"! It belongs today to the age of innocence! The pages of music are before me as I write and as clear as a child's mind. Debussy's technic is no longer inexplicable. As for his idiom, one realizes now several perfectly obvious derivations. Franck is not absent, nor Wagner, nor the presence of that Massenet who, said Romain Rolland, slumbers in the heart of every Frenchman. So that, where material and workmanship are concerned, there is no longer mystery concerning the music, or certain of its relations to the immediate past. And yet, even without the orchestra, etched by the black and white tone-colors of the piano, the piece renews its magical and pagan spell. I am confident that this unique composition will hold its place, and—God grant it!—be forever mysterious to us. There will be regressions from Debussy and from the school of musical impressionism which he is supposed to represent. But in the first place, as I have implied, this apparently nebulous music is written with astounding precision and a wholly concealed but iron substructure of form; and secondly, a work of great genius, whatever its school or period, lives. This languorous score, with its indolent flute, its shimmering horns and harp, its nostalgia for a beauty that cannot exist in the world of living, will remain with us, and place us ever the more in debt and homage to that honored master who, for us, transfixed the dream and preserved it forever in little black notes on music paper.

•

Three Nocturnes for Orchestra

I. "Nuages" ("Clouds")
II. "Fêtes" ("Festivals")
III. "Sirènes" ("Sirens")

Debussy was supremely the artist capable of selecting the instant of pure beauty and transfixing it on his tonal canvas for eternity. The "Nocturnes" for orchestra, of which the first two are most frequently played, are impressions, almost painter's impressions, of nature. In the first Debussy seeks, in his own words, to contemplate "the unchanging aspect of the sky, with the slow and solemn passage of the clouds dissolving in a gray vagueness tinged with white." The harmonic and orchestral method is close to that of the painters who so daringly, for their period, mixed conflicting colors and secured marvelous vibrations of light. Even so does Debussy employ discords which, melting the one into the other, give us the impression of lucent sonorities. Watch for two of his most beautiful tints at the beginning of "Nuages," when the higher wind instruments of the orchestra begin a weaving figure and against them is heard the rich,

[224]

reedy, languorous tone of the English horn, set like a gorgeous ribbon of color against the undulating background of the other instruments. Gradually, after one vista and another, the vision recedes, and the tone fades almost imperceptibly into silence. Incidentally, the woodwind figure from which "Nuages" is constructed is note for note the same as an accompaniment figure in one of the late songs (the third song of the cycle "Without Sunlight") of Mussorgsky, a composer whom Debussy admired and carefully studied, and to whom he owed much.

* * *

I have remarked upon Debussy's impressionism and its analogy to the methods of painters of his earlier years. But he never abandons creative logic. And so, in the second piece, "Fêtes," passages which have apparently no relation to anything heard before are actually very original and imaginative transformations of themes already heard in "Nuages." It is also true of Debussy that his orchestration is as distinctive and varied as his methods are economical. The scoring of "Nuages" is in complete contrast to that of "Fêtes." The second Nocturne evokes "the restless, dancing rhythms of the atmosphere, interspersed with abrupt scintillations. There is also an incidental procession—a wholly visionary pageant—passing through and blended with the argent revelry; but the background of uninterrupted festival persists—luminous dust par-

ticipating in universal rhythm." Mr. Havelock Ellis
might have called this piece "The Dance of Life."
We distinguish, first, a dazzling play of rhythm, and
occasional scraps of the freest and happiest melody
in the world floating through it. At a certain point,
after a pause, a march-like accompaniment begins on
the harp. Over this sound faint fanfares, which come
nearer, mount to a refracting climax and pass by,
after which the dance of the particles of light is resumed, with the little fragments of wanton song.
Goethe speaks, in the prologue to "Faust," of the
"thunder-march" of the sun through the skies. So
this march of the sun-god thunders through Debussy's
orchestra and passes on its way.

*　　*　　*

" 'Sirens': the sea and its innumerable rhythm; then
amid the billows silvered by the moon the mysterious
song of the Sirens is heard; it laughs and passes."

Debussy asks a chorus of eight female voices, which
sing, without words, an undulant melody derived
from the theme of the first Nocturne, "Clouds." One
of the secrets of the music is the extreme simplicity
of its basic material. Two notes that rise or fall a tone
are the elements from which Debussy derives his
tonal structure. This idea, which would threaten
monotony, is unfolded in terms of inexhaustible
beauty. There was probably an analogy in Debussy's
mind in this sameness, almost monotony of subject-

matter, and its infinite variety of presentation, with the recurrences and ever-fresh miracles of nature herself. Different harmonies give various tonal backgrounds to the motive, which is the last word in simplicity. This motive is also varied rhythmically; various rhythms which it has generated are combined and contrasted. Someone said of Debussy that he was not only a composer but a de-composer. He meant the composer's tendency to boil down an idea to its fewest notes, to reduce a chord to its merest essentials, and to centralize his development about this essential simplicity. Other composers piled up themes and motives. Debussy sets musical particles free; he often seems to stand aside and regard with affection and worship their apparently careless play, and joyous obedience to basic laws. Apparent inconsequence of movement is a fascinating characteristic of his music. And so with this score. The listener is not aware of craft, and he is not surprised when the voices of the sirens fall upon his ear. This music is the fresh inspiration of a young poet. In a later perspective of Debussy's art it is seen to be the genesis of certain fundamental ideas, particularly that of the two-tone figure that he later expanded with such astonishing mastery in the pages of the score of "La Mer."

●

"La Mer," Trois Esquisses Symphoniques

("The Sea," Three Symphonic Sketches)

I. "De l'aube à midi sur la Mer" ("From Dawn till Noon on the Ocean")
II. "Jeux de Vagues" ("Play of the Waves")
III. "Dialogue du Vent et de la Mer" ("Dialogue of Wind and Sea")

There is, there always must be, a dividing line between the illimitable designs of nature and the necessarily established confines of any art. In music a point of nearest fusion between man's symbols and nature's designs seems to have been reached in Debussy's extraordinary symphonic sketches of the sea.

This music, in some respects the product of the most finished art, is in others the reflection of the inner and sensuous existence. That is an existence much older and in many respects of a profounder wisdom than the one of the conscious intellect. Debussy's perception of the sea has the natural clairvoyance of instincts as fresh as those of an animal, combined with the subtlety of the ancient culture of which this composer's art is a flower. One hearkens to the eternal ebb and flow of the waters, with their capricious swirlings, and whisperings, and treacherous calm, and inhuman play. There are reflected the constantly changing lights and colors of sea and sky. To it all there is no beginning and end, and no human story, no moral, no philosophy—only the enigmas of nature and beauty.

We do not know the moment and the thought which led Debussy to consider the sea as a subject for his musical inspiration. But this must have been just the release that he required at the time. What other idea would have offered as free play for his imagination and his special artistic resources? Here was the place to modulate as freely as he pleased, to assemble and mingle and disperse rhythms as fluctuant as those of the elements, and to utilize all the tone-tints of his orchestral palette. At an earlier period this invitation of the sea would have been artistically dangerous; in which case Debussy would probably have been wiser than to attempt it. "Sirènes," with all its freshness and charm, is a pretty picture in a frame beside "La Mer." In that work Debussy undertook something more vast and perilous. But the moment had come for the greater adventure. He entered upon it with inquisitiveness. Had there been within him more powerful and chaotic forces he might have been destroyed by this fusion with nature. Instead, he was cool enough, and sufficiently limited, to give us an unforgettable portrayal of the sea, drawn to his own scale. He was sufficiently sensuous, while remaining the observant Frenchman, to yield himself voluptuously to the sea's embrace, and put down just what she whispered in his ear, in terms of a liberated yet marvelously ordered music.

The movement, the undulation of tone, begins as mysteriously as the echo in a sea-shell. The ocean stretches indolently in the sun. Winds whisper and waves curl. The mood becomes more exultant and tumultuous. Cries of exultant spirits sound from the deep. Debussy does not concern himself with melodic lines, which would be so definitely out of place here. He utilizes fragments of harmony and little melodic figures, submerged in the interlacing rhythms and surges of the orchestral tone. You would say that he was more concerned with the glint and refraction of light on a wave than with methods of thematic development, yet the piece has sequence and organism. Toward the end a chorale is intoned by wind instruments under the clamor of the rest of the orchestra—the chorale of the depths which, with imposing splendor, returns in the last movement.

The middle movement of this symphonic structure takes the place, in a general way, of the scherzo of the symphony. It is a capricious dance of elements, a sport of wind and spray. The last movement is a gustier and wilder ocean, with a deeper pulse and menace. Debussy uses his scale of whole tone intervals, of which he was fond, with special results in this movement—in wild upward-rushing figures, and harmonic crashes, and in a broad figure that wonderfully reflects the surge and motion of the great white-maned horses of the sea. In a moment of lull and mystery a siren voice calls from very far away, and the cry is repeated, always more insistently and voluptuously. Rapid rhythmic figures and fanfares are counterpoints to the reappearance of the majestic chorale of the first movement, and an unusual harmonic conclusion is suggestive of the ever-enduring sea.

Some could say that Debussy's harmonic scheme, which seems so irregular, was really one of the closest interrelations, that there was a gravitation of shifting harmonic bodies about a central key. Specialists could argue that matter from the analytical systems of different schools of musical thought. More indisputable, and not less magical in this score, is Debussy's peculiar use of wind-instruments. That is unique, and is a principal source of the music's spell. The sonorous proportions of the modern symphony orchestra are a little too heavy on the string side to give these effects the proper measure of distinctness. It is when the string choir is reduced a little in its numbers that the wind parts are thrown into the proper relief. Once, owing to the accident of a small platform for a large orchestra, the writer heard "La Mer" done with a relatively small string choir. The effect was one of unforgettable strangeness and mystery.

●

"Iberia": Images for Orchestra, No. 2

I.   "Par les rues et par les chemins" ("In the Streets and By-ways")
II. "Les Parfums de la nuit" ("The Fragrance of the Night")
III. "Le matin d'un jour de fête") ("The Morning of the Festival Day")

It was for years the custom of critics to designate Debussy as a tonal impressionist and harmonist of peculiar sensitivity, and, having thus pigeonholed his style, turn complacently to other matters. They had not learned, or they had chosen to forget, that this most fastidious of workmen was deeply averse to saying the same thing twice, and that he was always seeking new aspects of beauty.

In "La Mer" (1905) Debussy had attempted and succeeded in an expression which marked the possible limits of impressionism. Composing "Iberia" (1909), he turned from this method to a harder and more precise style. He remains the tone-painter and worshiper of nature, but his manner of coloring is now that of the "pointillistes," who painted with a multitude of fine points rather than with free brush strokes and manipulations of color. The score of "Iberia" is very detailed and exact if examined closely, and in its development it is the most symphonically conceived of all Debussy's orchestral pieces. But stand off a little from this tone-picture. Listen from a distance: the sum of its details will be atmosphere and color planes of vivid and exotic hue.

The work is also a triumphant vindication of Debussy's purposes in that, despite the employment of symphonic devices, it is admirably free of conventions of the German school. Nowhere did he more conclusively than in "Iberia" expound a doctrine of development which liberated and followed the inner urge of the musical idea itself, instead of forcing that idea into a preordained channel. And never had he been more close-knit in the exposition of his thought.

How much happens in these three pieces! How logical their sequence and melodic relations to each other! The poetical scheme is the thought of the day, with its light and movement giving place to the perfumed and mysterious night, and the night leading, in turn, to the break of dawn, the stirrings of life, and the brilliancy and commotion of the Fair. In the first movement basic motives are laid down with the finest coördination and craftsmanship. The piece opens with a flourish of pulsatile instruments and pizzicato strings, with certain scintillating accompaniment figures, and a shrill ditty played in the reedy register of the clarinets. This scrap of melody might sound from any corner or roadside of the Spanish land. It returns in many and astonishing transformations in later pages. So, for that matter, does other thematic material laid down as part of the ground plan of the score. Confused calls and sounds are borne forward on robust rhythms, and seem to ring and intermingle in the clear air. The end of this movement is especially poetical. It is shadowed and vague like the falling evening and the melancholy distances of the sky.

The second movement is the apostrophe to the summer night of the exhaling flowers, the soughing breezes and the "large few stars." Free preluding introduces a habanera figure whose derivation can be traced back to the first movement. The motive pervades the orchestra. The instruments create a moonlit haze of tone and from far away sounds a horn with the melody of a tender song which is but another transformation of the clarinet motive of the opening. A recurring harmonic suspension is aquiver with the night's magic. There are effects of an unprecedented and inexplicable beauty. Who, for example, would suppose that the intermittent cluck of a xylophone would have anything to do with the spell and the passion of a summer night? It has precisely this potency at the hands of Debussy. He uses different scale formations, and there is a passage as chromatic as Wagner. The transporting song of the horn now sweeps passionately in muted strings. A hush falls upon the orchestra, and from far away sounds the faint tolling of bells. . . . The morning breaks. The orchestra flashes color, and one hears the plunking of guitars. Shrill wind-instruments add their notes. An amusing episode comes when, with another thematic transformation, the first violin, solo, saws extravagantly, for all the world as some fakir or mountebank might fiddle and clown it for a group that hailed the performance with shouts of laughter. All is song, rhythm, sun. A master holds out both hands to life.

RICHARD STRAUSS

1864–

Tone-Poem, "Don Juan," Opus 20

CONTEMPORANEOUS with Debussy was his complete antithesis, Richard Strauss. He is descended of Berlioz of the program symphony, Liszt of the symphonic poems, Wagner of the music dramas. He was not so much a revolutionist in his methods and idioms as he was a flaming temperament, a modern intellect, and an astonishing development of his age. He is a symphonist, a realist and dramatist in one. He was late in turning to the stage, but was expressing drama and psychology before that time in a series of symphonic poems that shook the world.

After years which have made the music thrice familiar and exposed certain banalities, I am taken aback, whenever I hear it properly performed, by the fierce onslaught of the opening measures of his "Don Juan," the first of the tone-poems in which Strauss unmistakably revealed his genius. Before this there was no such intrepid and sensual music, or music of such torrid, and lush, and violent orchestration. "Don Juan" was composed in 1889. It will soon have its

[235]

fiftieth anniversary, which is a long time in the modern tonal art. In that time purists and pundits have been telling us that the works of the vulgar and sensational Strauss could not live. Every decade they have been critically buried. But while critics were advancing excellent reasons for Strauss's artistic demise, and declaring the esthetic unsoundness of his program music, Strauss was creating an art of an astonishing and irresistible power. Before "Don Juan" he had composed copiously in various traditional styles, and learned the technics of his business. He had produced one tone-poem on the subject of "Macbeth," a combination of Brahms and certain fragmentary prophecies of the Strauss to come. But the real release occurred when Strauss's nature had ripened, when contact with literature quickened his creative consciousness, and he had found the courage uncompromisingly to take his own path. The subject of Lenau's "Don Juan" seems to have made a powerful appeal to his imagination. With this symphonic poem a long pent-up force broke loose—erupted like Vesuvius. What came out was not all pure flame: there were rocks and mud. But *Don Juan* himself did not set out on his adventures with more defiance and lust of conquest than the youthful Strauss who portrayed him.

To gain all that can be gained from this music it is necessary to take into account Strauss's conception. This *Don Juan* is not the mere rakehell sensualist of the Spanish fable. He is, after all, an intellectual hero. He is the dreamer as well as the voluptuary, the adventurer who seeks in all women the ideal. The quest is fruitless; disgust and contempt for life grow upon him until existence is intolerable, and in despair he allows himself to be stabbed in a duel. This is the character projected by the Austrian poet, Nicolaus Lenau, and it is this conception which provoked the proud, delirious and bitter music of Strauss.

In the opening passage the knight is before us, imperious, defiant, aflame with the lusts of life. There are two episodes of love music. Officious commentators, whom Strauss has not taken the trouble to contradict, find in these episodes the figures of legendary ladies—*Donna Anna, Donna Elvira.* Or what would you? No matter. The headlong music changes its course. With sweeps of the harp, some bell-like tones of the celesta and a phrase of the solo violin, the music becomes nocturnal; the *Don* woos impetuously. His passion smolders and flames. The amorous song mounts to a palpitating climax, but the mood soon passes. "I flee from surfeit and from rapture's cloy." New fires begin to flare in the music; and now, over a deep murmuring accompaniment of strings and horns the oboe sings a song of the world well lost. An effect of suspended harmonies holds the spell to the last possible moment, when it is dispersed by *Don Juan's* second theme, a lordly phrase, one of the most magnificent Strauss ever conceived, given to

six horns in unison. To this motive of the horns other
instruments make agitated rejoinder. But the re-
doubtable theme rings out again with knightly scorn.
Now Strauss flings his colors like a pot of paint on the
orchestral canvas. In one place the *Don's* horn theme
is caricatured in silly fashion by the glockenspiel.
This is the place, according to self-appointed eluci-
dators, where, after riotous misbehavior, *Don Juan*
falls intoxicated to the ground, and there pass in his
confused brain vague images of earlier experiences
and the fleshly phantoms he pursued. The moment
when the commentators fancy the knight unconscious
is the passage in the orchestra when fragments of the
love themes are heard over long-sustained tones of the
low instruments. This is the moment that precedes the
true climax of the tone-poem. Once more the orchestra lashes itself to a frenzy, when suddenly, just as it
seems that the tidal wave of tone must crash and
overwhelm us, it is transfixed and frozen into silence.
There is a catastrophic pause. A veil seems to fall over
the instruments. Through this veil of tone cuts a dissonant trumpet note—the mortal thrust, the death of
the dream, the end of every man's desire. Perhaps this
is the most remarkable page of the whole tone-poem.
The conclusion is laconic, tight-lipped. There is no
wild complaint, no hysterical wailing. Only abandonment of life.

It is strange music from a young man of twenty-
four. The energy and color of the score could be ex-

plained by the fire of the youthful revolutionist Strauss was when he composed this work. But the ending, with its striking negation of feeling, was a new note in music of the modern German school, and perhaps harbinger of the negativity that has characterized the later period.

•

Tone-Poem, "Death and Transfiguration," Opus 24

The tone-poem "Death and Transfiguration" was first composed and then explained in a poem by Alexander Ritter, now printed in the score. Whether Strauss's meaning when he composed the music was precisely the same as Ritter's poetical explanation is an open question. That the poem is authorized by the composer; that it gives us a true interpretation of the essential things that Strauss meant is self-evident. But this music of memories and agonies and aspirations would speak for itself without any program.

Ritter's poem, in substance, pictures a man lying half-conscious in a dim, necessitous little chamber, fever-tossed, awaiting death. A candle, flickering as uncertainly as the life that is in him, casts wavering shadows, and the book of life is turned back page by page as the exhausted man dreams. He dreams of his childhood, of the battleground of youth, the torn banner of the ideal carried dauntlessly forward; the hopes, futilities, illusions that beset him, and the remorseless foes that confront him at every turn of the upward path. And death strikes, and out of blackness and void rises the music of apotheosis.

Some call Strauss's introduction realism, for it depicts the fluttering breath, the weak pulse of the erstwhile clamoring heart, and the weary sigh of the sufferer—this sigh being transformed later and fused into the hymn of victory. But if this is realism it is part of the necessary background for a drama of the utmost intensity and pathos. A new theme is associated with memories of childhood. Death makes a furious onslaught, and Strauss's fiery scroll unfolds a picture of the terror and riving of the flesh, and prophecy of the transfigural moment to come. Death retreats for a moment. Thoughts of childhood recur, and then, with horn-calls, of the challenge of life. A thrilling page is that in which the music mounts with desperate gallantry till it encounters the "Halt!" of the trombones, and the orchestra falls back and fathers its forces again and again against the inexorable foe— man or destiny, as it may be. And now, from the blazing vortex, is flung again, in golden chords, the prophecy. There a last struggle, and the darkness of the Pit. In the orchestra is chaos and void, until the chant begins to rise slowly, with other themes twining about it, and is taken up by instrument after instrument, and choir after choir of praise. Instrumental colors like intensifying light accumulate, and finally there is a blinding climax, one of the greatest in modern orchestral music. James Huneker once spoke of the final E-flat chord of Strauss's "Heldenleben" as of unexampled gorgeousness. That chord is dull and thick by the side of the rainbow colors with which Strauss ends "Tod und Verklärung." This, bear in mind, is one of his early tone-poems. It has not such distinctive workmanship or harmonic quality as "Till Eulenspiegel" or "Don Quixote," but it has simple, majestic, diatonic themes which bring Strauss near to Beethoven's simplicity and heroism. It is a work of such compassion and faith that it stands alone among Strauss's scores, and in these respects superior to most of the others.

●

"Till Eulenspiegel's Merry Pranks (according to the ancient rogue's saga)" in Rondo form, Opus 28

Who was *Till Eulenspiegel?*—or *Ulenspiegel,* as the Flemings called him. He is a figure of the ages which created a *Faust* and a *Don Juan* and other half-mythical characters which symbolize aspects of the soul of man. He is the imp of fantasy and the perverse. There are histories of *Till.* There is even a tombstone at Mölln, near Lübeck, crowned by *Till's* armorial bearings, which are an owl and a looking-glass (Eulenspiegel: owl's glass). But the tombstone is of the seventeenth century, and *Till* is believed to have died of the plague somewhere about 1350. There's another tomb at Damme. It has designs long believed to indicate *Till's* interment at that spot. But the design on the tomb is not that of a looking-glass at all. It is the emblem of a desk surmounted by a book. The tomb is that of one Van Varlant, poet and Recorder, who died in 1301, highly honored by the townsfolk. There is an owl, to be sure, but that is merely tribute to the man's learning. So there you are! When and where *Till* was born is doubtful, but one thing is certain: his spirit is deathless.

How did *Till* get his name and reputation? Perhaps because of his malicious jesting at the expense of his fellow-man. For there is a German proverb which says: "Man is as little conscious of his own faults as an owl or an ape, looking into a mirror, is conscious of his ugliness." *Till*, they say, was a wandering mechanic who lived by his wits, turning up in every town and city. He made himself out to be whatever the situation required—butcher, baker, wheelwright, joiner, monk or learned metaphysician. He was a lord of misrule, a liar and villain, whose joy it was to plague honest folk and play foul jests upon them. He pillaged the rich, but often helped the poor. In Charles de Coster's "Legend of Ulenspiegel and Lamme Goedzek" he is the soul and savior of the Netherlands, bleeding under the incredible atrocities of the Duke of Alba. In the German folk-tales he is hunted by an incensed community, captured, tried before a tribunal and condemned to death. But he always escapes. Strauss, apparently, hoists him up on the gibbet, and the suggestion of this moment in the music drew snorts of indignation and accusations of "realism" from the more ponderous and unimaginative of the composer's critics. Their indignation would have delighted the knave of legend, as it must have caused a sardonic grin to illuminate the countenance of Eulenspiegel Strauss. He could have quoted Wilde: that where some people catch an effect, other people catch cold. If the tone-poem means anything but beautiful music, it means that *Till* is immortal, that his spirit eternally triumphs, though bourgeois and Philistines rage never so furiously together. For *Till* is freedom and fantasy; his is the gallant, mocking warfare of the One against the Many, and the tyranny of accepted things. He is Puck and Rabelais, and there's quicksilver in the music.

The piece begins with a theme worthy of Mozart, an introductory phrase which is as the beginning of a fairy tale—Strauss's "once upon a time" (1).* Then *Till's* horn theme scampers through the orchestra (2). Some sharp chords and the rogue's off on his deviltry. What is it all about? When the piece was first performed at Cologne in 1895 Strauss said that if he were to utter the thoughts that certain passages suggested to him, "they would seldom suffice and might even give rise to offense." And in the music there are bursts of

* See page 158.

coarse and outrageous laughter. But, regarding this work as others, Strauss has permitted certain commentators, more or less self-appointed, to act as Official Spokesmen for him. These gentlemen have furnished a "program" generally accepted as casting light upon the music. According to this, the rogue rides his horse full tilt into the market-place. He upsets the stalls, and the market women yell at him. You hear the clatter in the orchestra—Strauss uses a rattle. *Till* disguises himself as a monk. He makes love to a fine lady and is furious at his rebuff—a transformation in the minor of his horn theme (7). He rages at those who mock him. Once he is nearly caught, and badly frightened—you hear his choking cries. But in a moment he's away, his terrors forgotten, his joyous singsong echoing from far off in the ears of his pursuers (8).

Till's adventures multiply; his impudence knows no bounds. Finally he is brought to justice. Sentence is pronounced with pontifical majesty and gloom. The knave grimaces and whines his innocence. "No mercy," thunder horns and trombones and drums (12), and up he goes, to eccentric skyward leaps of the clarinet and gurglings of wind-instruments. And he's done. His adventures are over! (13). But was it *Till* who died? Strauss's epilogue reassures us. The magistrates destroyed the effigy, not the living soul, and the lovely theme of the introduction returns, opening like the petals of a flower in the orchestra. *Till*, acknowledging no master but the beauty that beckons from over the horizon, lives still in the hearts of men— once upon a time and forever.

Are we justified in reading into Strauss's music anything of an ulterior or philosophic meaning? There is that in the score which implies more than a purely musical or decorative intent. *Till* runs amok in the old tales and in Strauss's orchestra, which echoes laughter but also pathos, and sarcasm, and even savage revolt. I think we have here something of a commentary upon life, its ironies and tears, and homage to the triumphant and uncapturable thing that soars and sings high up and beyond prison bars, or scaffolds, or even the excellent rulings of worthy people.

The score is an epitome of finished and resourceful workmanship, stemming, as it does, almost entirely from the two themes associated with *Eulenspiegel*. Of these themes the transformations and developments are extremely interesting, whether they are viewed as parts of an organic symphonic structure or as showing the capacity of a great master to reveal his motives in different lights. Of the first theme the variants shown on the accompanying chart are (3), (4), (6), (8) and the last five measures of (13). Each one of them is a triumph of invention and esprit. Number (8) is especially impudent and ingenious—Eulenspiegel Strauss thumbing his nose at the world! Transformations of the second theme—the horn theme—are (7), the two last measures of (8), and the lower line of

(11), wherein versions of both themes are combined. Illustration (5) is a delightful new theme, or episode, in the folk-vein of much of the music, a vein so delightfully resumed in the second episode relating to *Till's* escape (9). (12) is the portentous pronouncement of the tribunal. These last three fragments are episodic and receive little development. All the rest of the score springs from themes (1) and (2)—the result of consummate technic, imagination and musically creative genius.

Not a note could be added to or taken from this score without impairing its proportions. It is the expression, not merely of individual genius, but of the soul of a people. Their humor, their homely wisdom and deep and unconscious poetry are in it. And there is the good laughter of Master Rabelais, and the good savor of the earth from which oak and violet grow.

•

"Also sprach Zarathustra" ("Thus spake Zarathustra," freely after F. Nietzsche), Opus 30

"Also sprach Zarathustra," the tone-poem that Strauss composed after a reading of Nietzsche's rhapsody, is a flight of unparalleled audacity which may outlast nearly everything the composer has produced, and may, on the other hand, be consigned with other intellectual excreta of the nineteenth century to oblivion. It is a huge, Gargantuan, misshapen thing.

[246]

Resting rather crazily on the earth, it towers toward the stars. Composing it, Strauss was a real Nietzschean. You feel a Nietzschean afflatus, a Nietzschean scorn, laughter, passion in every measure of the score. Whatever its curious weakness or discrepancies may be, it is indeed the Superman of which it speaks. The greater part of it is certainly tremendous music, perhaps the most daring in its quest of any Strauss wrote. There are those, it is true, who find this tone-poem a thing of bombast and caricature—one of Strauss's greatest mistakes. And he has made many. Ah, but it is glorious, if it is a mistake, to make a mistake like this!

James Huneker said that Zarathustra should be played to an audience of poets and madmen, who alone would understand it. The opening, the sunrise music, made Philip Hale, when he first heard it, think of "the portals of eternity, swinging slowly asunder." Others have made particular fun of Strauss's attempting "to express philosophy in music." (As if the basis of three-quarters of the music of Strauss's whole century had been anything but philosophy!) What is obvious is that Strauss would never have written this extravagant and incandescent work without the stimulus of Nietzsche's thought.

Here the Superman sings of himself deific. Man has emerged from the womb of nature, from the shadows of his spiritual past and the shackles of his Liliputian present. He affirms proudly his lordship of earth and heavens. He has shaped for himself a morality at one with that of nature, and has asserted, once and for all, the supremacy which it is his obligation to fulfill "in the fusion of God, world and ego." Strauss composed his music in seven months in 1896. He said to Otto Floersheim: "I did not intend to write philosophical music or to portray in music Nietzsche's great work. I meant to convey by means of music an idea of the human race from its origin, through the various phases of its development, religious and scientific, up to Nietzsche's idea of the Superman. The whole symphonic poem is intended as my homage to Nietzsche's genius, which found its greatest exemplification in his book, 'Thus spake Zarathustra.' "

A simple little thing.

The piece is scored for an enormous number of instruments, which may be cited as example of how the orchestra expanded from the days of Beethoven to those of Strauss, after which period it was to become smaller again. The orchestra is as follows: for the woodwind, piccolo, three flutes (one interchangeable with a second piccolo), three oboes, English horn, two clarinets in B-flat, clarinet in E-flat, bass clarinet, three bassoons, double bassoon; for the brass, six horns, four trumpets, three trombones, two bass tubas; for the strings, sixteen first and sixteen second violins, twelve violas, twelve violoncellos, eight double-basses; organ; two harps; for percussion instruments two kettledrums, bassdrum, cymbals, triangle, glockenspiel and a low bell in E. On the fly leaf of the score is an excerpt from Zarathustra's "Introductory Speech" as follows:

"Having attained the age of thirty, Zarathustra left his home and the lake of his home and went into the mountains. There he rejoiced in his spirit and his loneliness, and for ten years did not grow weary of it. But at last his heart turned—one morning he got up with the dawn, stepped into the presence of the Sun and thus spake unto him: 'Thou great star! What would be thy happiness, were it not for those for whom thou shinest? For ten years thou hast come up here to my cave. Thou wouldst have got sick of thy light and thy journey but for me, mine eagle and my serpent. But we waited for thee every morning and receiving from thee thine abundance, blessed thee for it. Lo! I am weary of my wisdom, like the bee that hath collected too much honey; I need hands reaching out for it. I would fain grant and distribute until the wise among men could once more enjoy their folly, and the poor once more their riches. For that end I must descend to the depth: as thou dost at even, when sinking behind the sea, thou givest light to the lower regions, thou resplendent star! I must, like thee, go down, as men say—men to whom I would descend. Then bless me, thou impassive eye, that canst look without envy even upon over-much happiness. Bless the cup which is about to overflow, so that the water golden-flowing out of it may carry everywhere the reflection of thy rapture. Lo! this cup is about to empty itself again, and Zarathustra will once more become a man.'— Thus Zarathustra's going down began."

The score opens with perhaps Strauss's greatest and simplest page, that which portrays the sunrise. A low C is sustained for many measures by the organ and double-basses. From this dark and vague background strides the flashing trumpet, with the great motive of the whole tone-poem. It is made of the simplest possible intervals, which are basic in our musical system—the three notes, C, G, C—the first, fifth, and first repeated in the octave. Huneker calls attention to the fact that this interval of the fifth holds within itself both major and minor tonalities, which play in this cosmic introduction. The motive itself obviously was associated in Strauss's mind with the thought of Nature, or the World-Riddle, as certain Germans have put it, and the simple gigantic motive pervades the whole score.

The orchestra responds to the trumpet-call as if the earth, with a great sigh, were awakening from her slumber. The drums begin to thunder, the trumpet-calls are repeated, and the response is more resounding. The summons is flung out for the third and last time. The whole orchestra answers, with the full C major chord, so scored that it is as a blinding radiance of light. This is Zarathustra's salute to Nature and the Universe, and now begins his "going-down."

Various captions in the score associate the music with phases of Nietzsche's poem. The first of these is "OF THE BACK-WORLD DWELLERS." They are the ones who were victims of the old religions. "Then," says Zarathustra, "the world appeared to me the work of a suffering and tortured God."

The great chord of the sunrise music is relinquished by the orchestra to the organ, and then is suddenly stopped. For an instant the ears are deceived, quite as the eyes would be if a bandage had suddenly been put over them after they had gazed straight into the light. There seems for a moment to be no sound (and in fact there is only a softly rolling drum). Then the listener becomes aware of a trembling and stirring in the shadowy depths of the orchestra. Over the tremolo of muted 'cellos and basses sound pathetically a dialogue of low wind-instruments and a phrase of plain-chant, and from the heart of the darkness rises a hymn of worship and supplication. But the soul of man is not appeased. The hymn ends and violins sweep upward with the lyrical theme of

"THE GREAT YEARNING." "O my soul," said Zarathustra, "I understand the smile of thy melancholy. Thine over-great riches themselves now stretch out longing hands! . . . And, verily, O my soul! who could see thy smile and not melt into tears? . . . But if thou wilt not cry, nor give forth in tears thy purple melancholy, thou wilt have *to sing*, O my soul!" Two phrases are associated here. One an ascending motive of wide intervals, announced by 'cellos and bassoons, the second the theme of *sehnsucht*, of longing for the Ideal, played in thirds by the violins. This is answered doubtfully and mysteriously by condensations of the great Nature theme that seems to echo through space, and by another phrase of the plain

[251]

song, marked "Magnificat." The hymn is heard again. Under it a new turbulence is felt, which gains increasing mastery and leads with a sweep into the music

"OF JOYS AND PASSIONS." The new motive, of a proud curve, is developed with great richness of counterpoint, and stress and pull of the different voices against each other, when suddenly the trombones and tubas pronounce the stern and powerful motive, sounding majestically through the orchestral turmoil, against the swirl and sweep of the melodies that wail overhead. What the precise connotation of the phrase was in Strauss's consciousness we had better not be too officious in deciding. Let us call it a motive of Inquiry. With its very impressive appearance the music subsides from a mood of turbulence to one of reminiscence and melancholy, when Zarathustra, wandering among the tombs of his ancestors, sings his

"GRAVE-SONG." This, significantly enough, is an aftermath, a kind of codetta, sounded first in the pale tone of the solo oboe, of the theme of "Joys and Passions." The instrumental voices moan and converse with each other. The music dies away as Zarathustra turns to science for answer to the Riddle of life.

"OF SCIENCE." The great Nature-theme is now transformed into a tortuous and complicated double fugue which winds through many keys and sounds all the tones of the chromatic scale. But this is not long tolerated. The course of the fugue is interrupted by a return of the mounting sensuous melody of "the great longing"—the soul's ideal—and there is mocking laughter, and trilling of the strings, and sweeps of the harp. The Inquiry theme is bandied about and gibbered by various instruments. When the fugue is resumed its counter-subject is the Inquiry theme, and this is the music of

"THE CONVALESCENT." "Zarathustra jumped up from his couch like a madman. He cried with a terrible voice . . . and behaved as if someone else was lying on the couch and would not get up from it . . . he fell down like one dead, and remained long like one dead. At last, after seven days, Zarathustra rose on his couch, took a red apple in his hand, smelt it, and found its odor sweet. Then his animals thought the time had come for speaking unto him. . . . 'Speak not further, thou convalescent one! . . . but go out where the world waiteth for thee like a garden. Go out unto the roses and bees and flocks of doves! But especially unto the singing birds, that thou mayest learn *singing* from them. . . . Sing and foam over, Zarathustra, heal thy soul with new songs. . . .' Zarathustra lay still with his eyes closed, like one asleep, although he did not sleep. For he was communing with his soul."

The fugue advances mightily to its solution with various motives in counterpoint, and all sorts of rhythmic devices and reckless play of horns and trumpets against the subject. Over a tremendous pedal point, brass instruments march upward. At the sum-

[253]

mit of their progress comes the proclamation confounding in its splendor: simply the statement, against
resounding fifths, with all the power of which the
orchestra is capable, of the three notes of the Nature-
motive—as if Nature herself made this final and
crushing reply to all attempts of men to unriddle her
mystery.

After a pause a dialogue of instruments begins, followed by an amusing suggestion of the twittering of
birds, joyous leaps of an octave in the highest register
of the trumpet, seven-league strides of the strings,
and mocking laughter. This prepares for the

"DANCE SONG." Nietzsche tells us that Zarathustra walked out in the sun, through forest and
meadow. Some dancing girls were dismayed by his
grave mien, but he reassured them. "How could I, ye
light ones, be an enemy unto divine dances? . . . He
who is not afraid of my darkness findeth banks full of
roses under my cypresses . . . And I think he will also
find the tiny God whom girls love best. Beside the well
he lieth, with his eyes shut. Verily, in broad daylight
he fell asleep, the sluggard . . . Be not angry with me,
ye beautiful dancers, if I chastise a little the tiny God
. . . True, he will probably cry and weep; but even
when weeping he causeth laughter! And with tears in
his eyes shall he ask you for a dance; and I myself shall
sing a song unto his dance."

Huneker called the "Tanzlied" a scarlet dance.
What we hear, truth to tell, is a rather commonplace

Viennese waltz strain. But I think that it behooves us, in this place, to be charitable. Do you remember the story of the Juggler and Our Lady? The Juggler at the fair wanted to render fitting homage to Her blessed name, but he knew no proper religious cere- monial, or even the right way of praying. Wherefore he pulled out his kit, and sang and capered his best, as he often had done to the satisfaction of the peo- ple at the fair. The monks of the neighboring ca- thedral thought this blasphemy and were for punish- ing him. But the statue of the Blessed Virgin moved and protected the boy, thus making it known that his tribute was acceptable in Her sight. And so with Strauss the composer, and the inadequate material that he sometimes incorporates in his symphonic arch. If we separate the dance motive from its context in the tone-poem, it can appear commonplace enough. If we recognize, on the other hand, Strauss's spirit and objective, and observe the magnificent working out which follows, we will be fairer to him and to ourselves.

The solo violin takes the dance theme, over an ac- companiment played by the woodwind and made from the Nature-motive. Almost continuously, from this point on, the dance rhythm obsesses the orches- tra. There is a momentary lull, now and again, while serene and lofty thoughts are uttered. One of these moments—indeed, the turning point of the tone- poem from the thought of the problematic past to that of the future of release and light—is the solo of the horn, with a new phrase in a major key, derived from the music "Of joys and passions," a phrase as tranquil and exalted as Beethoven. Thereafter the dance rhythm gathers strength and momentum. It bears upon its crest motives which have preceded— that of laughter, of joys and passions, of Zarathustra's quest. The vast orchestra becomes corybantic. The supreme moment arrives when, over the pounding drums and violin figures which leap upward as though they would scale the skies, the great bell begins to toll for Zarathustra's midnight song of triumph. Overhead, with frantic exultation, the trumpets scream a version of the horn-motive of salvation. This cry is answered, antiphonally, by the lower brass instruments as the bell tolls on. Twelve times the bell strikes and Zarathustra sings his triumphant song— Nietzsche's "Song of the Night Wanderer," which afterward he called "The Drunken Song."

ONE!

O man, take heed!

TWO!

What saith the deep midnight?

THREE!

"I have slept, I have slept!

FOUR!

From deep dream I woke to light.

FIVE!

The world is deep.

SIX!

And deeper than day thought for.

[256]

SEVEN!

Deep is its woe—

EIGHT!

And deeper still than woe—delight!

NINE!

Saith woe: 'Vanish!'

TEN!

Yet all joy wants eternity!

ELEVEN!

Wants deep, deep eternity."

TWELVE!

With the last far-off reverberation of the bell, the orchestra takes on colors like those of a rainbow sky. The strings breathe the motive of the Ideal. This motive ascends. Mystical chords high in the registers of the woodwind are as receding stars. But the riddle is not solved. The tone-poem ends enigmatically in two keys, the Nature-motive plucked softly by the basses in its original key of C—and above the woodwinds, in the key of B major. The unsolvable end of the universe: for Strauss was not pacified by Nietzsche's solution.

●

"Don Quixote": Fantastic Variations on a Theme of Knightly Character, Opus 35

It was said that after the transcendentalism of Zarathustra, Strauss, composing "Don Quixote," was mocking himself. Certainly he caught and has nobly

[257]

conveyed, not merely the humor, but the humanity and pity of Cervantes's tale. Like the author, the composer has pictured for us two kinds of men, and opposed interpretations of existence—*Don Quixote*, the impractical idealist, and *Sancho Panza*, the realist—he who of all men may be the most blind!

It may be admitted that this is the limit of program music. Whether, if the score were not provided with explanations endorsed by the composer, we would all give it the same interpretation is much of a question. But that would also be the case with much other music of a dramatic kind. Strauss's progress from a composer of symphonic program music to a composer of music-dramas is apparent in every score that came from his pen. "Don Quixote" is, from one point of view, such literal music as to be almost visual—"moving pictures for the ear," as a German musician once remarked. But it is also music of astonishing delineation, an epitome of thematic development, modern tone-painting and psychological commentary combined."

The structure of the score is that of a theme, or rather themes, and variations. The two principal themes are those of the *Don* and *Sancho Panza*. Other themes which fill out the canvas and complete the characterization are manipulated with dazzling imagination and technic.

Strauss's introduction pictures *Don Quixote* reading his books of chivalry, waving his sword, fighting

[258]

imaginary foes, going mad, and preparing for his ad-
venturous quest. You hear also the cheerful and innoc-
uous voice of *Sancho Panza*. The ten variations suggest adventures of the pair. The final pages speak of
the noble renunciation and humility with which the
Don, his illusions gone, his pride shattered, his dreams
turned into vain and empty things, faces at last the
truth, and gives up the ghost, with the last failing
note—a slide downward—of the solo violoncello.

The introduction, announcing all the thematic material and transforming it as the *Don* broods on chivalry, is long, ending with trumpet-calls, and a pause
which leads to the first variation. The second variation is a famous passage, for which Strauss has been
much censured on the ground of realism where the
orchestra imitates the baa-ing of sheep. The *Don* sees
the flock of sheep as the hosts of great *Emperor Alfan-
faron,* and, charging, puts them to flight. The commotion, the baa-ing of the sheep are clearly audible.
Considerably later on is another device of realism
which will serve as a landmark—a screamingly extravagant page. This is the seventh variation—the ride
through the air. The *Don* and *Sancho* are supposed to
be seated, after the episode of the novel, on wooden
horses, blindfolded, and are given to believe that they
are riding through the air. Strauss here uses a wind
machine, which whizzes and whirrs, in combination
with vaulting scale passages for flutes and other instruments, and a persistent drum-roll. The themes of

the *Don* and *Sancho Panza* are heard, whirling heavenward in the blast. But they never leave the earth, as we are reminded by a low D, to which certain of the orchestral instruments stick right through the variation. These places are mentioned as landmarks.

The variations in order are as follows:

I. Knight and squire set out on their quest, talking of chivalry. The *Don* attacks the windmills. A slide of the woodwinds, a whack of the drum, and he falls.

II. The victorious battle with the sheep.

III. One of the noblest places in the score when, after some supposedly skeptical remark of *Sancho Panza,* the *Don* waxes eloquent on the subject of chivalry. The orchestra shimmers color, the strings sing a transformation of the knight's theme and a phrase of the ideal with a nobility that makes my throat tighten every time I hear it. The passage, which follows the sheep cries, may be recognized as a long variation that mounts to the climax with the violins rapturously repeating a high A-sharp at the climax.

IV. The adventure with the penitents. A whining choral is played by wind-instruments. The knight, believing these are villains and robbers, attacks them. They knock him down, then proceed prayerfully on their way.

V. *Sancho*, having helped his master to rise, sleeps. The *Don* holds armed vigil, and his supplications are rewarded by the vision of *Dulcinea*. She appears to him as a vision accompanied by crazy cadenzas of the harp. Few pages of the tone-poem mingle more touchingly the sublime and ridiculous, while the 'cello rhapsodizes over somnolent harmonies of wind-instruments—the sleeping *Panza*.

VI. The meeting with the country wench whom the *Don* believes to be *Dulcinea*. She comes along the road with a tamborine, present in the orchestra, and a ridiculous tune. *Sancho* guys his master, telling him that this really is *Dulcinea*. The *Don* concludes that she has been victimized by an enchanter.

VII.   The ride through the air.

VIII. The journey in the enchanted bark. Knight and squire jump into an empty boat, ride tipsily downstream, and are upset. I am sure that I hear, at the end of this variation, with the pizzicato notes of stringed instruments, the drops of water falling from them, as well as the little prayer that Strauss has penned—thanksgiving of the travelers for their safety.

IX. The combat with the two magicians; they are two harmless monks, whom the knight puts to flight to a contrapuntal passage given the bassoons.

X. This variation is brilliant and warlike. It is the fight with the knight of the White Moon. He is none other than *Quixote's* neighbor of the home town, *Señor Carasco*. The conditions of the conflict are that if the *Don* is defeated he must do the bidding of the conqueror. He is unhorsed and sent home. A shepherd's horn is heard as the *Don* and *Sancho* ride slowly homeward, and the orchestra wails over the doleful drums. And then the farewell and benediction! The solo 'cello is the knight's voice, his farewell to life, and commendation of his soul to God.

Does this fulfill its purpose as music, or merely by the power of partly realistic suggestion? This is surely true: that while, if uninformed, we might not find in the variations the exact incidents they are supposed to depict, we can hardly fail, if our ears and minds are open, to feel tenderness, humor, ironical caricature and pathos in the music. Nor is anything more impressive than the progress of this music as it evolves from the astonishing fantasy and complexity with which Strauss pictures the glowing disorder in the *Don's* mind, and the wealth of imagery and expressive device in the variations which follow, to the utter simplicity and humility of the last pages, when everything but the truth and the wistfulness of the truth has dropped away from him—the dauntless quest ended, the weary traveler home. For this page alone we would owe Strauss much. And who are we, after all, to question the sources of his inspiration? A novel by Cervantes, a folk-tale or poem by Nietzsche— what matter? Strauss, whether or not his esthetic is faulty, has given us prodigiously of music.

•

"Ein Heldenleben," Tone-Poem, Opus 40

"Ein Heldenleben"—"A Hero's Life"—like Strauss's "Symphonia Domestica," contains provokingly good material. Provoking because this is a case of aggressive egotism, because its hero is Strauss himself, who hymns in a fifty-minute tone-poem his own greatness and the pettiness of his enemies. Who are they? Presumably the critics! It is a sweet revenge, since, if fair-minded, they must praise at least the major part of this tonal autobiography. It is not Strauss's first attempt at self-glorification, for his second opera, "Feuersnot" (Need of Fire), has in transparent guise a certain *Richard*, a magician, for its hero, who brings a backward community to heel by the fires of his genius. The opera strutted an unsuccessful hour, but the tone-poem survives, and makes one of the brilliant pages of modern music. "Heldenleben," a regular *Pickelhaube* rhapsody, brags and swaggers to such warm and virile melody, such rhythmic energy, such vitality and splendor of counterpoint, that the listener must cry *"Kamerad"* before it is over, and confess that this, the most conceited of all the Strauss scores, is by and large a compelling achievement. "Ein Heldenleben" has six main divisions, labeled in the scores as follows:

1. *The Hero.* The Hero's theme mounts superbly from the registers of the orchestra. It is a broad, sinewy theme, developed with polyphonic magnificence

[263]

for many pages. This is Strauss's delineation of a heroic character—written, as it turns out, in the same key as Beethoven's "Eroica" symphony. Whether a hero with less self-esteem would perceive a less gratifying image in the mirror is a question, and if we were discussing the heroism of Beethoven's "Eroica" we would be talking of something else again. Strauss's hero is of grosser fiber, and it is of himself and not human destiny that he sings. But here is an astonishing amount of sheer music, sure-footed if not eagle-winged. The first part of the symphonic poem comes to an end on a great reverberating chord—that of the "dominant seventh"—as the hero sets out on his adventures to the sound of trumpets and banners flung to the breeze.

2. *The Hero's Adversaries*. They are a petty, snarling, malicious crew. The instruments squeak and gibber. The hero theme is heard, as in lofty rebuke, and for a moment the foe is silenced.

3. *The Hero's Courtship*. The hero's helpmeet, whom he woos, is capricious. She is pictured by the solo violin. To her coquetries there are grave replies. The dialogue between the solo violin and other instruments becomes more tender as the orchestra with sweep of the harp releases the song. The world is forgotten until the spell is broken by the gibbering of the foe without, and the hero, his paradise disturbed, girds his loins for battle.

4. *The Hero's Battlefield*. Fanfares resound. Strug-

gle is waged without quarter. The whole percussive battery announces the onslaught. The hero theme and the theme of the adversaries clash. Not the least amazing feature of this tonal frenzy is the ingenuity with which Strauss contrives that the theme of the Beloved shall shine through the terrific din and the assault of choir upon choir and motive upon motive. The air is filled with mutilated fragments of motives. No such noisy and brutal thing had been done before in orchestral music, and it is extremely questionable whether anyone wants to see it done again. The din of conflict gives place to songs of triumph as the enemies are routed and run, howling like dogs, squealing like rats, their cries submerged in the chant of victory.

5. *The Hero's Works of Peace*. What are they? What but the earlier scores of Richard Strauss. Sailing along side by side, as effortlessly as cockleshells on a stream, are motives from the tone-poems "Death and Transfiguration," "Don Quixote," "Till Eulenspiegel," "Macbeth," "Thus Spake Zarathustra"; the first opera that Strauss wrote, "Guntram"; and one of the most poetical of all his songs, "Dream Through the Twilight." And it is serene, lofty, superbly coordinated music.

6. *The Hero's Release from the World*. Again the voices of the adversaries are heard, snarling in the tubas. There is orchestral remonstrance, and a change to a happier and more serene mood. The hero has renounced life and the illusions men hold dear. The

voice of the Beloved—the solo violin—is heard again. The ending sounds the motive of the sunrise music of "Zarathustra." The hero has glorified himself after the indisputable fashion of genius.

●

"Symphonia Domestica," Opus 53

It will be seen that Strauss's last important works for orchestra, before he turned with the operas "Salome" (1905) and "Elektra" (1911) to the theater, constituted tonal autobiographies, in two parts—Vol. I. "Heldenleben" (1899): the character, adventures, love, and creative achievements of the hero. Vol. II. "Symphonia Domestica" (1904): The hero's family life. We are thus permitted to conclude that after all and notwithstanding his earlier associations with the minds of Shakespeare, Lenau, Nietzsche and Cervantes, our hero found himself the best of company.

Strauss told a reporter in 1902 that his next tone-poem would illustrate a day in the family life. It would be a work "partly lyrical, partly humorous—a triple fugue, the three subjects representing papa, mamma and the baby." The prophecy came true. The "Domestic Symphony," Opus 53, "dedicated to my dear wife and our boy," was heard for the first time in America, the composer conducting, at the third concert of the Richard Strauss Festival, March 21, 1904, in Carnegie Hall. Europe did not hear the work till

Strauss conducted it the following June at Frankfort-on-the-Main. His score asks for an orchestra of 108 pieces.

This symphony is in one continuous movement, of which the subdivisions correspond roughly to those of the classic form. The first part unfolds the theme of the parents and the child, with some development. The second part, the scherzo, is the child at play, followed by a cradle song. The third part is the slow movement, an adagio, labeled in the score, "Doing and thinking. Love scene." The lively finale is a double fugue, extraordinary for the humor, vitality and virtuosity of the writing, based, as Strauss had told the reporter, on the themes of papa, mamma and the baby, and including other episodic ideas.

The husband has three themes, announced at the beginning, and in succession. They are marked in the score "Easy-going," "dreamy" and "fiery." There is a smaller theme, too, which the composer called "Mürrisch," that is to say, grumbling or peevish. The first theme is announced by the 'cellos; the second, the dreamy one, by the oboe; the grumbling and less important motive, by clarinets and bass clarinets, and the fiery theme by the strings. Then come the wife's themes. Her character is not as complex, or let us say as many-sided, as that of hero husband. Or has the composer underrated his spouse? Does he exclaim to himself, as a violinist who once burst, in a fine frenzy, into the office of a music critic, and unburdened his soul concerning his domestic problems, "I am an eagle; she is a wren"? The wife has only two themes of which the first and most important is given violins, flutes and oboes, and the second, a gentler phrase and more melodic, given to solo violin, flute and clarinet.

The introduction of the child's theme comes after preparation, and is sounded by the oboe d'amore, an instrument that fell out of general use after Bach's time, but has been revived occasionally in late years. It is an alto oboe. Toward the end of this part of the symphony Strauss has an ascending figure for clarinets and muted trumpets which he marked, "Just like his papa," and an answering descending figure, "Just like his mamma." This introductory section also publishes the bath music, a highly ingenious splashing and squealing which, repeated later on, is laughably realistic.

The child theme, in a new and lively rhythm, marks the scherzo. There is again reference to the bath. The cradle song, reminiscent of a phrase of the F-sharp minor Barcarolle in Mendelssohn's "Songs Without Words," is played by clarinets. The clock—in the orchestra, the glockenspiel—strikes seven and this marks the scherzo's end. The slow movement is the love scene and it is Strauss in an eloquent and melodic vein. At its close the glockenspiel strikes seven again, and all the instruments wake up. There is much fun and racket, and splashing in the bath. The music is full of energy, *riant,* bubbling over with life. Its complications are as nothing. Melody and counterpoint flood the orchestra, as if the composer's pen could not go fast enough, and there is very brilliant instrumentation. The child's themes sing rapturously through the hullabaloo, which becomes always merrier, till the piece ends with a shout of the husband's theme. The "Symphonia Domestica" is filled with Bavarian sentimentality, a certain heaviness, good humor, beer. Strauss has always had a vein of a certain native bad taste, which grew upon him in his later years. It is but the fact, however, to remark that while we might have been spared this exhibitionism, and the same gifts been put to more distinguished uses, we have here, again, some living music.

"En saga," Tone-Poem, Opus 9

THE "Saga" of Sibelius might well be associated in the mind of the listener with some ancient Scandinavian epic. It is dark, fantastical, fate-ridden in character. Every page carries the impress of the North. Notice the curious orchestral colors. The customary kettledrums are absent. A distant roll of the bassdrum and flickering figures of the violins, divided and subdivided among themselves, cast a mist over everything, a mist pierced momentarily by a flute and a flaring trumpet. A huge heavy theme lurches upward through the gloom. The music quickens, the orchestra shrieks and skirls. Later, accompanied by curious sighs of other instruments, the violins intone a monotonous barbaric dance theme. The instruments brood over these things. They rumble and growl, prophesying war. Before the final climax there is an eerie, wailing lament of the muted strings, a passage once heard, never forgotten. Then the orchestra gathers itself, girds up its loins, and leaps into a dance with knives drawn—lust of battle, glory of death. It is a return in

JEAN SIBELIUS

spirit to great days forever gone—when we were greater men. Yes! When I hear this music I avow a carnal desire to discard the soft fat ways of life; to set out in oilskins, or something, for somewhere, to discover at least a desperate polar bear bent on conflict! But seriously—who else writes such music today? In these pages Sibelius is the last of the heroes. The music rises to furious defiance. The end of it all is ghostly lament. A gong is used with extraordinary effect under pianissimo chords, remote from the key in which the piece opened. There is Styx-like blackness and cold; a last flicker of life in the ashes of a fire that flared for a moment in the world's Arctic night, and the indomitable rhythm of the war-dance.

●

Symphony No. 4, in A minor, Opus 63

I. Tempo molto moderato, quasi adagio
II. Allegro molto vivace
III. Il Tempo Largo
IV. Allegro

This symphony is one of the loneliest and most original of modern compositions. The earlier Sibelius symphonies are more romantic and picturesque than the later scores and are heroic and racial in character. Sibelius was then chanting sagas of the heroic age. But with his later symphonies we are witnesses of an astonishing metamorphosis. Sibelius is no longer writ-

[271]

ing in terms of ancestral memory. He is looking deep within himself. He is thinking and speaking out loud, amid solitudes. Here in this Fourth symphony a man broods alone. Like the Demon of Poe, he curses with the curse of silence. For, paradoxical as it may sound, there is *silence* in this music. It is indeed an older and more tried spirit which speaks here than the northern bard and revolutionist of the earlier works—a spirit which recoils upon itself; which, other than its constant communion with nature, knows no confidant. In these pages Sibelius emerges, lonely and incomparable, one of the deepest and most concentrated musical thinkers of our epoch.

The Fourth symphony is a series of musical ideas, boiled down to their sheerest essence, and there is no factitious allure about it at all. It is pure music, of the most transparent and unadorned kind. Sibelius's orchestra, from the full, sonorous symphonic panoply of the earlier works, has become comparatively a small one. Then there is the matter of harmony and form. Whereas in earlier works Sibelius accepted the harmonic and formal systems that he found at hand, and adapted to his own use, in the Fourth symphony he sets out upon a plan wholly his own. The technical procedure of the traditional symphony is for the greater part thrown to the winds, and this with an independence which can hardly be called courage, since it is so natural to the composer. He simply speaks out loud. If we who listen do not like it, all right. He has not even thought of that. For there is no defiance, no deliberate attempt to frighten the bourgeois in this work. Sibelius is simply himself, writing with a mastery and unconventionality which grow more wonderful to me every time I hear the work. For it is an unprecedented alembication, and a style highly modern in texture, which strikes like the arrow to the heart of the musical idea.

If you ask, "What do the different movements of this symphony mean?" the answer is music and states of the spirit not readily to be conveyed in words. The introduction of the first movement is one of the most original passages in modern music—and purest Sibelius. Then there is the capricious scherzo, with fragments of dance music, and, in the second part, a cry flung from instrument to instrument, and a sudden, abrupt end, as of a man too impatient with futilities to dwell longer upon them—or, incidentally, to complete his scherzo according to the dictates of classic form.

The slow movement is perhaps the greatest movement of the symphony, and this movement has dramatic as well as musical design. Its effect is this: the murmuring soliloquies of various instruments; then the hint, first by the stopped horns, of the theme which will gradually unfold itself in the orchestra; the recurrence of the murmuring voices; the theme returning in proportions continually larger and grander; at last the theme, in its complete form, striding from the depths of the orchestra, rising, over great choral harmonies of the brass, to its full stature of majesty and defiance; then sinking sullenly back, while a sustained C-sharp, and laconic pluckings of the basses, speak of man's defeat under skies which have become the ceiling of his despair. Sibelius's finale is a movement of restless energy, fitful gayety, protest; as when the great call of the solo trumpet is heard, over an accompaniment of strings which undulates like the sea; as when motives clash with each other, in dissonant counterpoint; and at last the desolate end—the descending motive of the trumpet, the wail of the oboe, the answering gray chords of the strings—always softer, grayer, till the music has vanished, like a gull in a misty sky.

PAUL DUKAS

1865–

"The Sorcerer's Apprentice"

(After a ballad by Goethe)   *searetso*

IT IS well that there was only one Debussy in France, else had we all become lotus-eaters! Paul Dukas's orchestral scherzo, "The Sorcerer's Apprentice," is a crackling Gallic joke. The ballad of Goethe affixed to the score tells an old and fantastical tale of the magician who was master of a broom which, by means of incantation, he could call to his bidding. Now one day, in the magician's absence, the rider of crocodiles, using the master's words, ordered the broom to become a pestle, and fetch him some water. It did so immediately, and continued to do so, though ordered to stop. In desperation, the fellow took an ax and split the pestle in two; but this made matters worse, for it divided in half, and each half fetched water, which flowed in a torrent. Suddenly the magician reappeared, took in the situation, uttered words that set things right, then vanished in displeasure and was never seen again. In Goethe's ballad these incidents are enacted by the Sorcerer and his Apprentice. The introduction, hinting at themes to come, including that of the Sorcerer's command, is mysterious. After a while three bassoons begin the farcical jumping motive associated with the unrestrainable antics of the broom. The music grows wilder, the orchestra rocks with the rhythm. At a climax the Sorcerer motive is proclaimed. There is a pause in the racket, but the movement is soon resumed, accelerated and set off with all sorts of ingenious instrumental devices. Torrents of tone are released; there is a resounding climax, greater than the first. Then the word of command sounds forth again, and this time in earnest. All is well, and there is a return to the quiet of the introduction. A capital joke, with echoes of other French composers, such as Gounod and Chabrier.

"Schelomo"

A VISITOR, one morning in 1916, to a small ill-furnished room on Lexington Avenue, New York City, was confronted by a man of less than medium height, with eyes that blazed beneath a fine forehead, and a mouth which was a crease of agony. The man was Ernest Bloch. After endless misfortunes he had come to America to conduct an orchestra for Maud Allan. The tour failed. He, fortunately, was left here stranded. It happened that the score he played me, shouting raucously as he assaulted a helpless and tinny upright piano, was that of "Schelomo." Yelling and pounding, he projected, composer fashion, his music.

No wonder the piano suffered, for this music is wholly orchestral in conception, and nothing less than many instruments could give it vent. The purple and gold of the instrumentation is setting of the somber reveries, the bitter complaints and prophetic denunciations of the solo violoncello. This solo instrument, with its rhapsodic song, is the voice of Schelomo. Schelomo is the Jewish name for Solomon, and it is of

Solomon in his glory, his wisdom and his disillusion-
ments that Bloch sings. In so doing he is expressing
the dreams of his own Hebrew race, and is the first
great Jewish composer to do so. There have been
other Jewish composers—many of them. Some were
minor figures, or at least figures historically unknown,
who contributed to the lore of Jewish religious or
folk-music. Others were famous men like Mendelssohn or Rubinstein, whose music, which might have
been grandly racial, was so tinctured and weakened by
conventionalizing European traditions that it lost its
spiritual identity, and was by so much lessened in
force and authenticity. Bloch's purpose is otherwise.
It is his desire to express not only himself but his race,
and he has done this in a manner which places him in
the front rank of living composers.

Only a few months before Bloch came to America
he had met in Switzerland the 'cellist Alexander Bar-
jansky, to whom the score of "Schelomo" is dedicated, and had seen a wax sculpture by the 'cellist's
wife, Catherine Barjanska, of Schelomo. A long-
bearded figure sits on the throne clad in royal robes
that cover the lower part of the body. The face is
very old and weary, with deep sunken eyes, hollow
cheeks and protruding temples. It is the King, weary
of life, weary of riches, weary of power. Inspired by
this sculpture, Bloch composed in a few weeks his orchestral rhapsody, in which, in the words of the Italian critic and musicologist Guido Gatti, "The violon-

'cello, with its ample breadth of phrasing, now melodic
and with moments of superb lyricism, now declama-
tory and with robustly dramatic lights and shades,
lends itself to a reincarnation of Solomon in all his
glory, surrounded by his thousand wives and concu-
bines, with his multitude of slaves and warriors behind him. His voice resounds in the devotional silence,
and the sentences of his wisdom sink into the heart as
the seed into a fertile soil; 'Vanity of vanities, saith
the Preacher, all is vanity. . . . One generation passeth
away, and another generation cometh: but the earth
abideth forever. . . . He that increaseth knowledge increaseth sorrow.' " Notice the strange instrumental
coloring, the wild outcries, alternating with deep
black shadows in the orchestra, from which, as from
utter solitude and darkness, there sounds the last solil-
oquy of the 'cello. This rich, blazing music is fairly
flung from the orchestra, and with what fury! At
last the passion is spent. The end makes one think of
Renan's speech at the funeral of Turgenieff, when he
spoke of those reveries which, through centuries, had
amassed themselves about that heart.

Bloch says of his music: "I am not an archæologist.
It is not my purpose to attempt a reconstruction of
Jewish music, or to base my work on melodies more or
less authentic. I hold it of the first importance to
write good genuine music, my music. It is the Jewish
soul that interests me, the complex, glowing, agitated
soul that I feel vibrating throughout the Bible: the

freshness and naïveté of the Patriarchs; the violence that is evident in the prophetic books; the Jew's savage love of justice; the despair of the Preacher in Jerusalem; the sorrow and immensity of the book of Job, the sensuality of the Song of Songs.

"All this is in us; it is in me, and it is the better part of me. It is all this that I endeavor to hear in myself and to transcribe in my music: the venerable emotion of the race that slumbers 'way down in our soul." And he said also that his setting of certain Psalms, his symphony "Israel," and his "Schelomo" for 'cello and orchestra, were highly representative of him, "because they come from the passion and violence which I believe to be the characteristics of my nature."

IGOR STRAVINSKY

IGOR STRAVINSKY

1882–

"Oiseau de feu" ("Bird of Fire")

ONE of the large number of scores called into being by Serge Diaghileff and his Ballet Russe, a score which introduced a new genius to the modern musical world, was Igor Stravinsky's ballet "Oiseau de feu" ("Bird of Fire"), the scenario based upon a tale of Russian folklore. This ballet was first performed in Paris in 1910. It is the first of the astonishing trio of compositions which placed Stravinsky, within a period of five years, in the position of the leading composer of his day. The other two were "Petrouchka" and "Sacre du printemps."

Two suites have been made from the music of "Oiseau de feu." The one mentioned here, the first, has six parts, but only three separate movements. The music in its original form accompanies dance and pantomime on the stage. The *Prince Ivan*, hunting, and wandering far, comes into the domain of an enchanter. The introductory measures of the suite consist in sinuous passages for the lower strings, chortlings of clarinets and bassoons, whispering arpeggios of harmonics by the violins, silver notes of the celesta scattered like delicate spray over the harmonies of the orchestra. Such is the musical depicting of the enchanted domain. The pace quickens, with capricious rhythms and curious instrumental effects, as the astonished prince observes from his hiding-place a marvelous bird, with wings of flame, which enters the garden and begins to peck at golden apples that grow on a silver tree. In sport the prince captures the bird, but, heeding its entreaties, releases it, retaining only a feather, which later proves a talisman in time of greatest need.

In the garden of the enchanted dwell captive princesses. The prince watches them dance. The dance of the princesses is gentle and grave. It is a "Korovode," or Russian round dance, preluded by a naïve little phrase on the flutes. The dance begins to the melody of an oboe accompanied by sweeps of the harp. Later the strings enter, warmly, tenderly—an adorable piece, made of the material of Russian peasant song. That is the second movement of the suite.

The sinister magician, *Kastcheï the Deathless,* who captured the princesses and turned rescuing knights to stone, appears on the scene. Warned by his diabolical instincts of the presence of an intruder, surrounded by his evil crew of monsters, freaks, Bobolochki, Kikimoras, and what not, he instigates a nightmare dance. I can say that I saw that dance, done by Diaghileff's superb interpreters: I saw it! I was there! You will infer the antics of the monsters by the wild shriek of the orchestra, and the savage, grotesque measures of the dance. In time, the *Fire-Bird* returns, to cast her spell of slumber on *Kastcheï* and his hosts, and rescue *Ivan* and his beloved. Thereafter veil-like harmonies descend upon the instruments. The harp commences a rhythmic accompaniment. The bassoon—an inspired tone-color in this place—sings the magic lullaby, a hypnotic song, enveloped in weaving harmonies of the upper voices of the orchestra.

The lullaby leads into the final movement of the suite. It is a transition of exquisite device. This finale celebrates the breaking of the magician's evil power, and the nuptials of the royal pair. The knights' images come to life, the princesses are free. *Ivan* and his beloved gaze into each other's eyes. A horn winds from far off over hills of dream. Its burden is an ancient Russian folk-tune. On the stage there are solemn preparations for the nuptials. The horn melody, repeated and variously transformed, takes on more splendor, the orchestra piling sonority upon sonority. The glorification of the song occurs when *Ivan* and his *Princess,* her white ermine robes extending the depth of the stage behind her, advance side by side to their happiness. The folk-melody is heard now in an odd rhythm and with clashing harmonies of the brass which suggest archaic pomp and the ringing of bells. There stand the pair, as beautiful as the dawn. The final chords are like gates that swing open to receive and protect them from evil.

●

"Petrouchka"

The exquisite and tender music of "The Bird of Fire" is that of Stravinsky's age of innocence. He quickly progressed to something quite different, a curious blend of Russian humanitarianism and the most sophisticated objectivity—the score of "Petrouchka."

Petrouchka is a doll, a puppet-like man. He is the superfluous one, and the helpless victim of a brutality he cannot combat. Paul Rosenfeld ("Musical Portraits") finds this figure to be "the man-machine seen from without, unsympathetically, in its comic aspect. . . . Countless poets before Stravinsky have attempted to portray the puppet-like activities of the human being, and *Petrouchka* is but one of the recent innumerable stage-shows that expose the automaton in the human soul. But the puppet-show of Stravinsky is singular because of its musical accompaniment. For, more than even the mimes on the stage, the orchestra is full of the spirit of the automaton. The angular, wooden gestures of the dolls, their smudged faces, their entrails of sawdust, are in the music ten times as intensely as they are upon the stage. . . . The score is full of revolutions of wheels, of delicate clock-work movements, of screws and turbines. . . .

And what is not purely mechanistic, nevertheless completes the picture of the world as it appears to one who has seen the man-machine in all its comedy. The stage pictures, the trumpery little fair, the tinsel and pathetic finery of the crowds, the dancing of the human ephemeridæ a moment before the snow begins to fall, are stained marvelously deeply by the music. . . . It has indeed a servant-girl grace, a coachman ardor, a barrel-organ, tin-type, popcorn, fortune-teller flavor."

Leonid Sabaneyeff, in his "Modern Russian Composer" (International Publishers, New York), says, somewhat devastatingly, that "the brightest place among Stravinsky's compositions belongs to 'Petrouchka.' Both his opponents and those whom he subsequently alienated were unanimous in admiration of this composition. Perhaps this very woodenness of the theme itself gave him an advantage, for one does not ever sense Stravinsky's soul in his music; he hides it painstakingly; perhaps he is a sort of Petrouchka himself, and instead of a life of the soul, he has only tricks and tin-foil magic. Perhaps, like Petrouchka, instead of blood he has *klyukva* (variety of cranberry juice), and instead of entrails, sawdust. This magician can occasionally make one believe that he is a great musician and make one overlook the inner chill of his creations, which have not been composed by thought and heart but by cold calculation and a hellish technic and the inventiveness of its 'inventor.' "

[285]

Another comment of a communistically inspired hue: "The ballet depicts the life of the lower classes in Russia, with all its dissoluteness, barbarity, tragedy, and misery. Petrouchka is a sort of Polichinello, a poor hero always suffering from the cruelty of the police and every kind of wrong and unjust persecution. This represents symbolically the whole tragedy in the existence of the Russian people, a suffering from despotism and injustice. The scene is laid in the midst of the Russian carnival, and the streets are lined with booths in which Petrouchka plays a kind of humorous rôle. He is killed, but he appears again as a ghost on the roof of the booth to frighten his enemy, his old employer, an allusion to the despotic rulers in Russia."

The scene is the Admiralty Square in old St. Petersburg, at the time of "Butter week" in the Eighteen Thirties. The rising curtain shows a crowd milling around the show-booths. There is dancing, laughter, horse-play. Two organ-grinders compete with each other, and are capitally taken off by the orchestra. The old showman, with his flute, comes before the people, assuring them by his gestures of an important spectacle. The curtains of the booths are yanked aside, and they reveal three life-sized dolls, figures which prance and cavort in a quick, mechanical way to the music. These dolls are *Petrouchka*, the poor foolish hero of the farce; the *Dancer*, and the *Moor*. *Petrouchka* loves the *Dancer*, but she is insensible to his advances, and, on the other hand, is much taken by

[286]

the swaggering, coarse, sensual *Moor*. And so the pup-
pets are set spinning, and one of life's little ironies, in
effigy, passes before us.

A roll of the drums and the scene changes to the
room of *Petrouchka*. He enters, distracted, consumed
with his desires and despairs. He rehearses steps and
gestures with which he hopes to impress the *Dancer*.
She enters, but is frightened by *Petrouchka's* eager-
ness, and soon leaves. The drum rolls again. We see
the room of the apish *Moor*. He is toying with a coco-
nut before which, since he can neither open nor understand it, he soon prostrates himself in worship.
Clad in his gorgeous uniform, he is lolling recumbent,
when the *Dancer* enters with her pirouette and her
toy trumpet, to coquette with him. The *Moor* watches
her, first with indifference, then complacency, finally
with greed. *Petrouchka* bursts in, to the annoyance of
the pair, and the *Moor* kicks him out for his pains.
The *Dancer*, with feigned reluctance, falls into the
arms of the *Moor* as the curtain falls.

Again the scene of the fair. The crowd becomes
more uproarious as evening gathers, and snow falls.
Dances by grooms and nurses. A lumbering bear is
depicted by the tuba in the orchestra. Drunken merchants reel in with gypsy girls on their arms; they
scatter ruble notes to the multitude. Suddenly there
are cries of consternation. From the booth, before the
alarmed crowd, runs *Petrouchka*, terrified and un-
armed, pursued by the *Moor*. The *Moor* quickly over-

takes and cuts him down. The puppet falls with an agonized squeak. The people do not understand. What has happened? The venerable showman steps forward. He reassures them. See! He picks up *Petrouchka;* sawdust falls out. This is not a living man, nor a human heart. Only a mechanism, with sawdust for a soul. Sometimes these mechanisms go wrong, and this one is in need of repair.

The show is over. Gradually the Square is emptied. The showman prepares to shut up shop and retire. But suddenly, over the roof of the booth, is seen *Petrouchka's* ghost, white-faced, with arms that wave in protest, like a crazy semaphore. Ghostly, too, is the commentary of Stravinsky's music.

Several interpretations of "Petrouchka" have been quoted; to any of them, or to some other one of his own, the reader is entitled. Its tragedy is the more gripping for its laconism. Let us admit nothing, lest we weep. The scenario of "Petrouchka: Scènes burlesques en four tableaux," is by Alexandre Benois. Subject and music appear to reflect the Russian nature. Gogol and Mussorgsky are there. Everything is reflected in the score with a sure and reckless mastery —the movement and tumult of the crowd; the gait and aspect of each leading figure; and the grotesque agonies of the helpless one. A shriek of two trumpets in different keys is the motto of *Petrouchka's* protest. The composition is permeated with Russian folk-melodies and also street songs marvelously treated. The technical virtuosity, in the combinations of rhythms and keys, is already breath-taking—I say "already," with thought in mind of the epochal "Sacre du printemps," still to come. The instrumentation has a new, acrid and kaleidoscopic glint. One would be tempted to say that the composer who could achieve two such manifestations within a period of two years as "The Bird of Fire" and "Petrouchka" could expect an unlimited future.

•

"Sacre du Printemps"

"Sacre du printemps" was an explosion, violent and terrifying and ominous, in the midst of an exhausted society. It was not only a sensation such as Paris (Théâtre des Champs Élysées, May 29, 1913) had not experienced for many years; it appears now almost as a pre-war token of catastrophe, and it was so potent and unshackled that it provided ideas for European music of the next two decades. This latter fact was amusingly evident in America, which was much longer than is usually the case in hearing a novelty by a European composer. The reason for the delay was the literal riot that occurred at the première of the "Sacre," which frightened our visiting conductors. In Paris the piece was greeted with hisses, cheers, and physical violence in the audience. Pierre Monteux, who conducted, though he became conductor of the

Boston Symphony Orchestra in the season of 1919–1922, waited until 1924 to present it to audiences of Boston and New York. The event proved that he need not have waited. The music, which he presented magnificently, was received with immense acclaim.

In the meantime, between 1913 and 1924, all sorts of new music had come over from Europe. Experiments with polyharmony, polytonality and with new rhythmic combinations astonished and captivated us. And then we heard the "Sacre du printemps" and knew at once that this was the treasure house from which Stravinsky's contemporaries, to the enrichment of their art, if not to the impoverishment of his, had helped themselves with both hands—and this with the air of those giving birth to new ideas. With "Oiseau de feu" and "Petrouchka" our young Russian had shown himself first a youthful promise and then a commanding talent; with "Sacre du printemps" he became the leading figure among the creative musicians of his epoch.

Sir Oliver Lodge said that there was sufficient energy in an atom, if released, to blow a battleship from its place in the ocean to a mountain-top. A portion of this dynamite seems to inhabit Stravinsky's score. Despite which, one can feel desolate in the presence of this sterile force, which is without the shadow of humanity, or the remotest suggestion of sentiment, and which, for lack of such fertilizing emotion, becomes perverse, exasperated, sadistic. The music then appears as the vicious outburst of an overstrained civilization. "The primitive man? The super-ape!" cried one of Stravinsky's colleagues. It is too soon to appraise this music, or even try to. It is also worth remembering that Stravinsky's emotion is not of the sentimental or romantic description, and that there is one passage, at least, in "Sacre du printemps" which grips us because of its half-articulate sadness and mystery. That is the introduction to the second part. There, in a strange iron twilight, the earth, helpless in its fertility, seems itself to fear and to lament the endless cycle of deaths and resurrections to come. Elsewhere is a super-dynamism, and a force, so to speak, partly chemical, partly physical, with very little suggestion of feeling, of which Stravinsky, anyhow, is intolerant. (At least in the "romantic" sense of the word.) The drums of the final pages, with their brutal and terrific impact, strike ears and nerves like bullets.

This is an interesting characteristic of the "Sacre": that whereas all the other ballet music that Stravinsky wrote is heard to the best advantage with the stage spectacle, the "Sacre du printemps," so far as any choreography thus far presented is concerned, is at its best in purely symphonic performance. Such an impression squares with remarks of Stravinsky himself. He told Michel George-Michel that the theme which made the basis of the composition came to him as a purely musical conception while he was writing the "Fire-Bird." (As a matter of fact, the precise notes of

the initial theme are contained in Mussorgsky's opera,
"The Fair at Sorochinsky.") Stravinsky continued:
"As this theme, with that which followed, was conceived in a strong, brutal manner, I took as a pretext
for developments, for the evocation of this music, the
Russian prehistoric epoch, since I am a Russian. But
note well that this idea came from the music; the
music did not come from the idea. My work is archi-
tectonic, not anecdotical; objective, not descriptive
construction."

According to this, then, story and choreography of
the ballet were superimposed, after the conception of
the music.

"The Consecration of Spring," in its official capacity, is concerned with prehistoric ceremonies held
by ancient man to make the earth fertile by the sacrifice of a human victim. The first part of the work
is called "The Earth's Fertility" and the second part
"The Sacrifice."

The slow introduction is supposed to imply "the
mystery of the physical world in Spring." The tone
color of solo bassoon, later combined with horn and
clarinets, has itself a hieratic quality. Wind-instruments predominate, a prophecy of Stravinsky's growing devotion to wood and brass, and in place of the
more pliant and illusory strings. The curtain rises, and
the rhythmic incantation begins. This is called in the
score the "Dance of the Adolescents." The accents are
vigorous and irregular. Youths and maidens stamp the

earth. The dance becomes more violent, and a part of this ritual is a mock abduction of a maiden. "Ronde de printemps"—"Spring Rounds." There is a pause, a breathing place, while a quaint theme sung in unison by clarinets and bass clarinets is accompanied by trills of the flutes. A solemn new rhythm, with strong and bitter harmonies, introduces another dance. The trumpets, with sharp, grinding harmonies, or poly-harmonies, chant a version of a theme already heard, a sort of primitive song of homage. Then come the "Game of Rival Towns" and the "Procession of the Sage," when an old white-haired, white-bearded man prostrates himself, and all kiss the ground and rise and dance to music of frenetic power.

The second part of the ballet begins with the music of groping mystery to which reference has been made. "Mystic Circle of the Adolescents": girls dance, and one of them is chosen for the sacrifice. There are pas-sages of "Glorification," "Evocation of Ancestors," "Ritual Performances of the Ancestors." Then a circle forms about her, the victim lashes herself to the final frenzy. The rhythms become convulsive, disintegrat-ing. She falls, to the beatings and shriekings of Strav-insky's orchestra. The score is a marvelous study in rhythmical and harmonic developments. While the music sounds, no one at all sensible to its force can doubt it. When it was heard in New York for the first time in 1924, there were reviewers who confidently and rapturously announced a new masterpiece for the ages, and few were the pens that restrained their praise.

Since that time Stravinsky has diverged almost completely from the tendencies that the "Sacre" represented. Is this an advance or a retrogression? The time has not come to attempt to answer that question, or, indeed, to put into the pages of a book gratuitous prophecy of the future that lies concealed in our period. *H F*